NO PART OF THIS BOOK MAY BE REPRODUCED SCANNED OR DISTRIBUTED IN ANY PRINTED OR ELECTRONIC FROM WITHOUT PREMISSION FROM THE AUTHOR

© Copyright 2020 by Coloring Hut – all rights reserved.

This Book Belongs to:

....

....

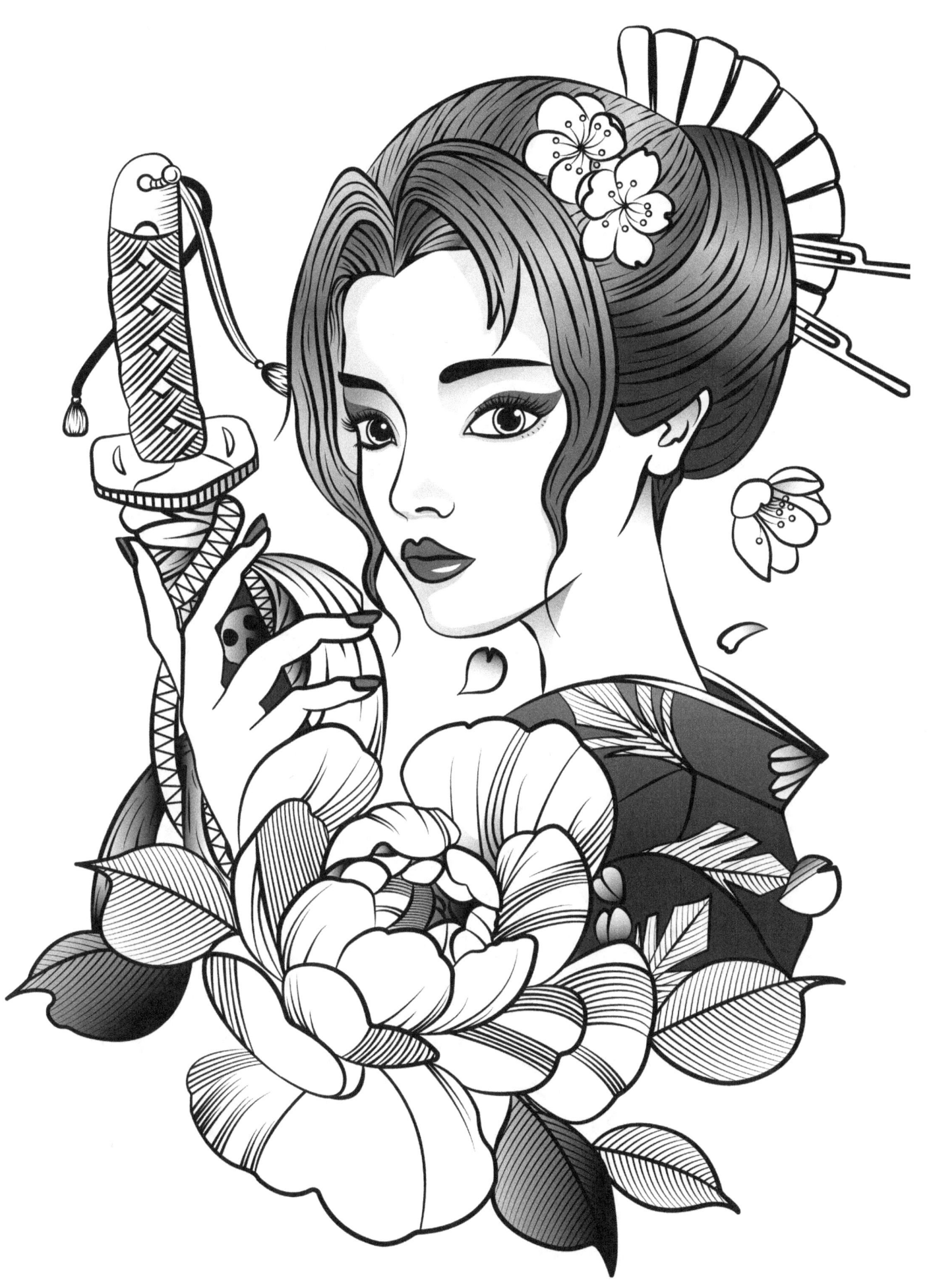

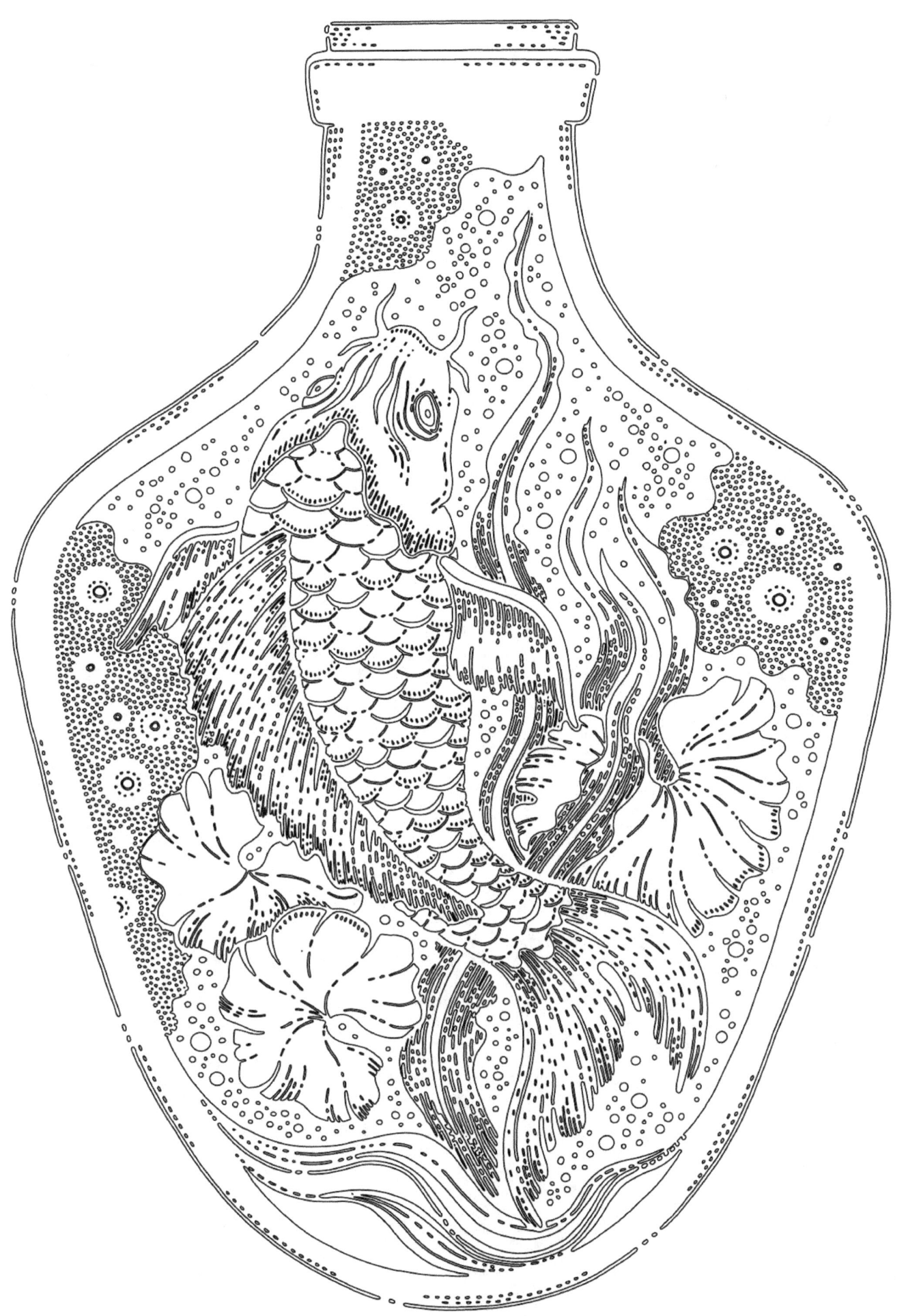

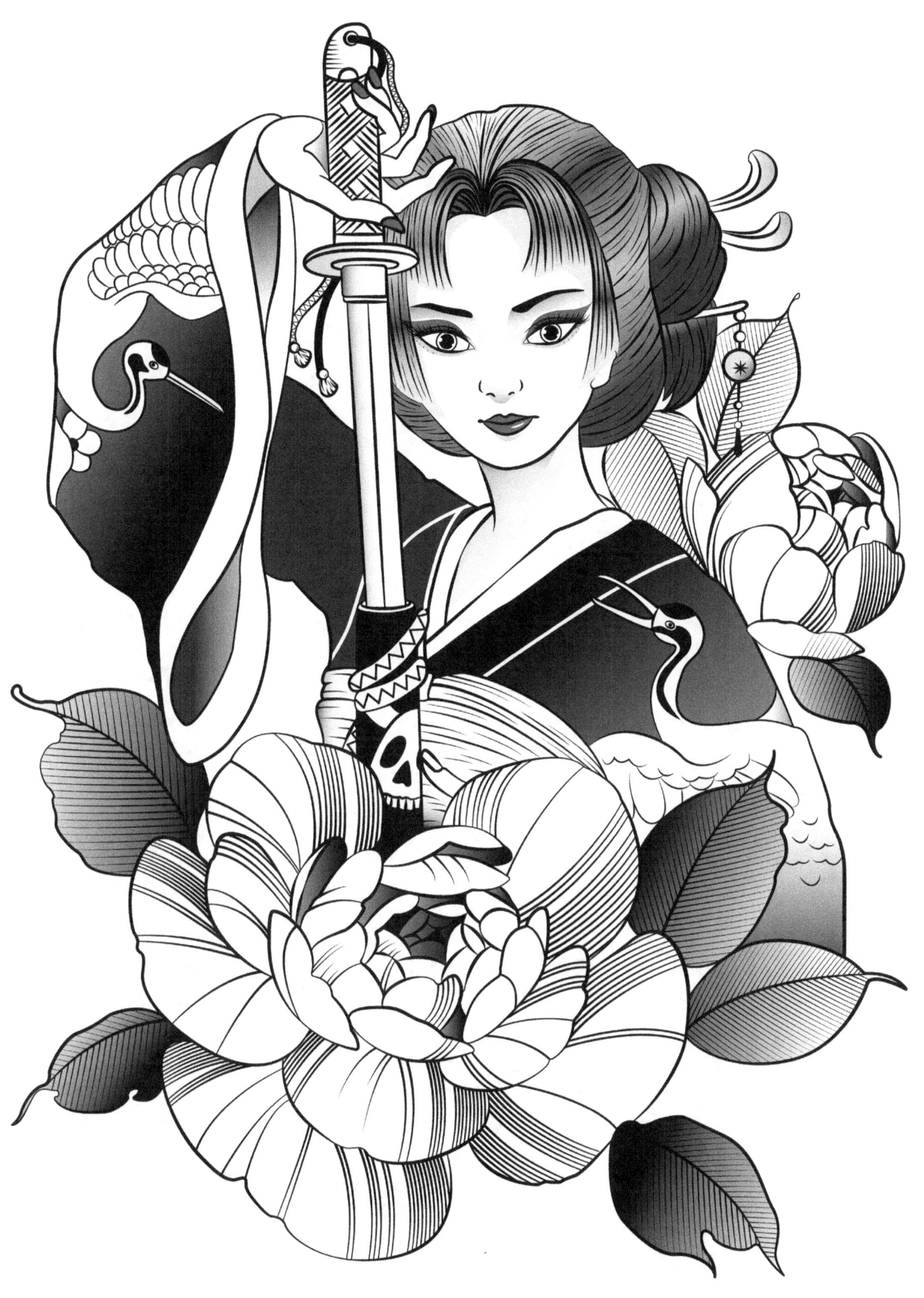

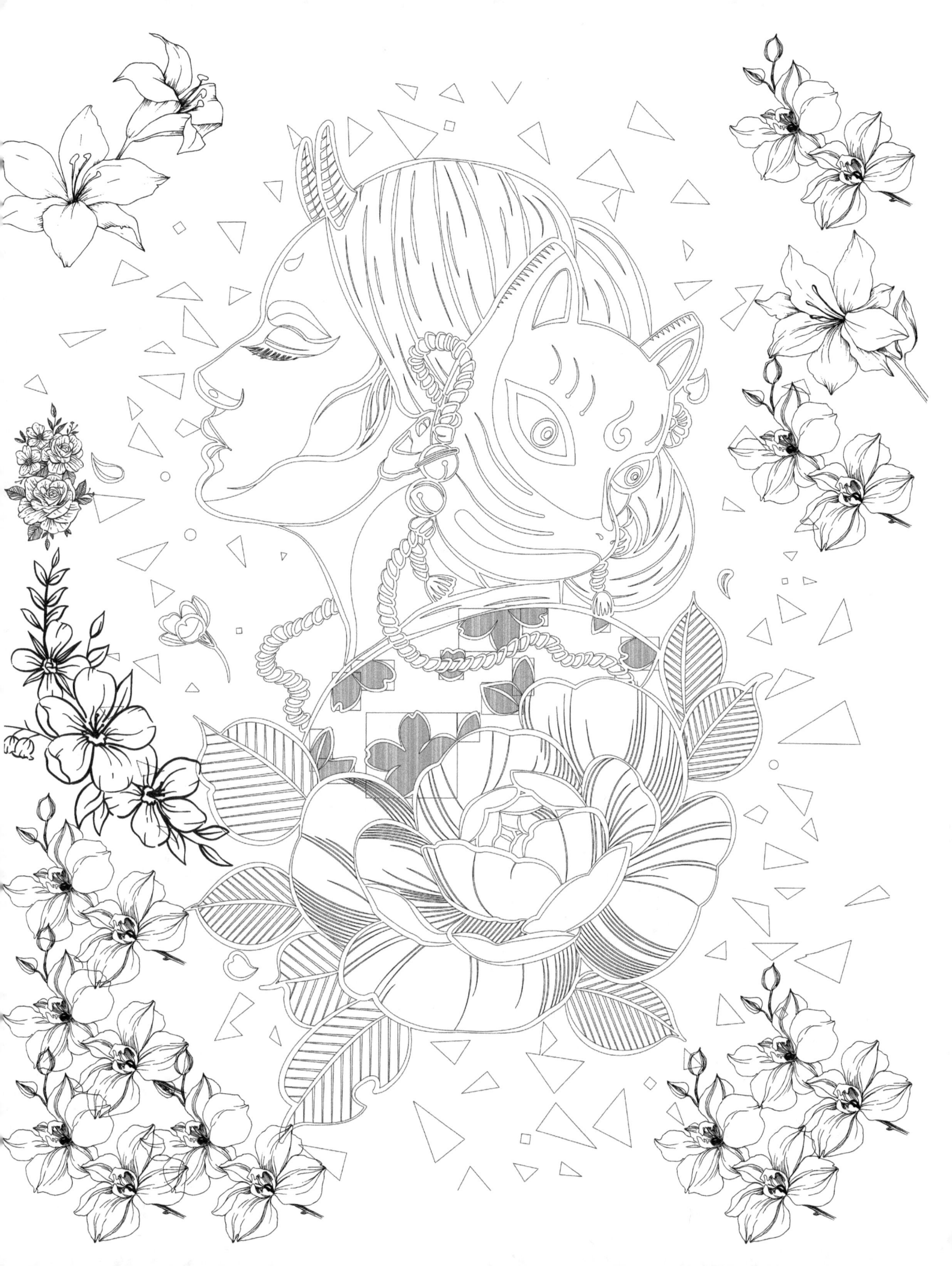

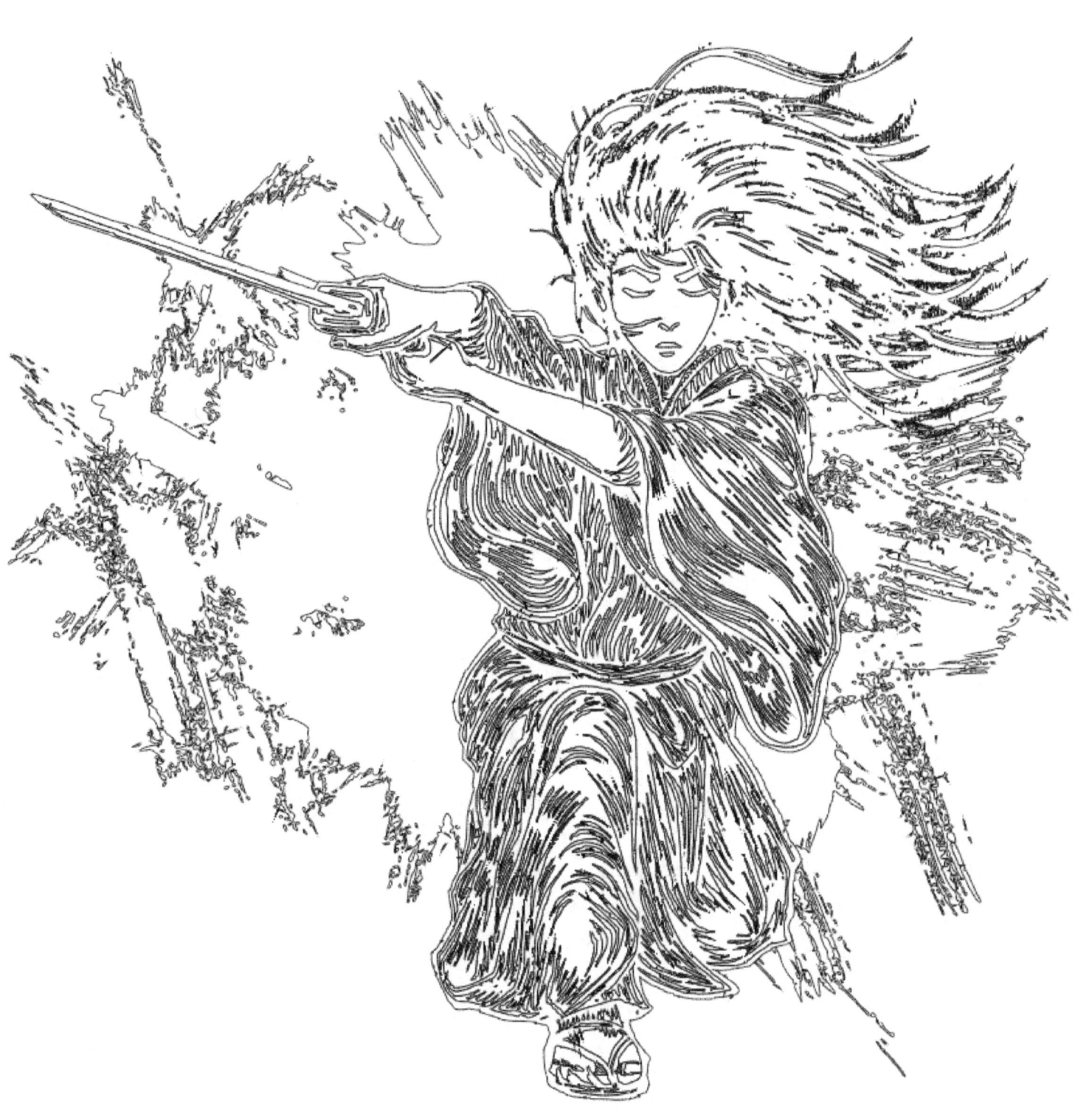

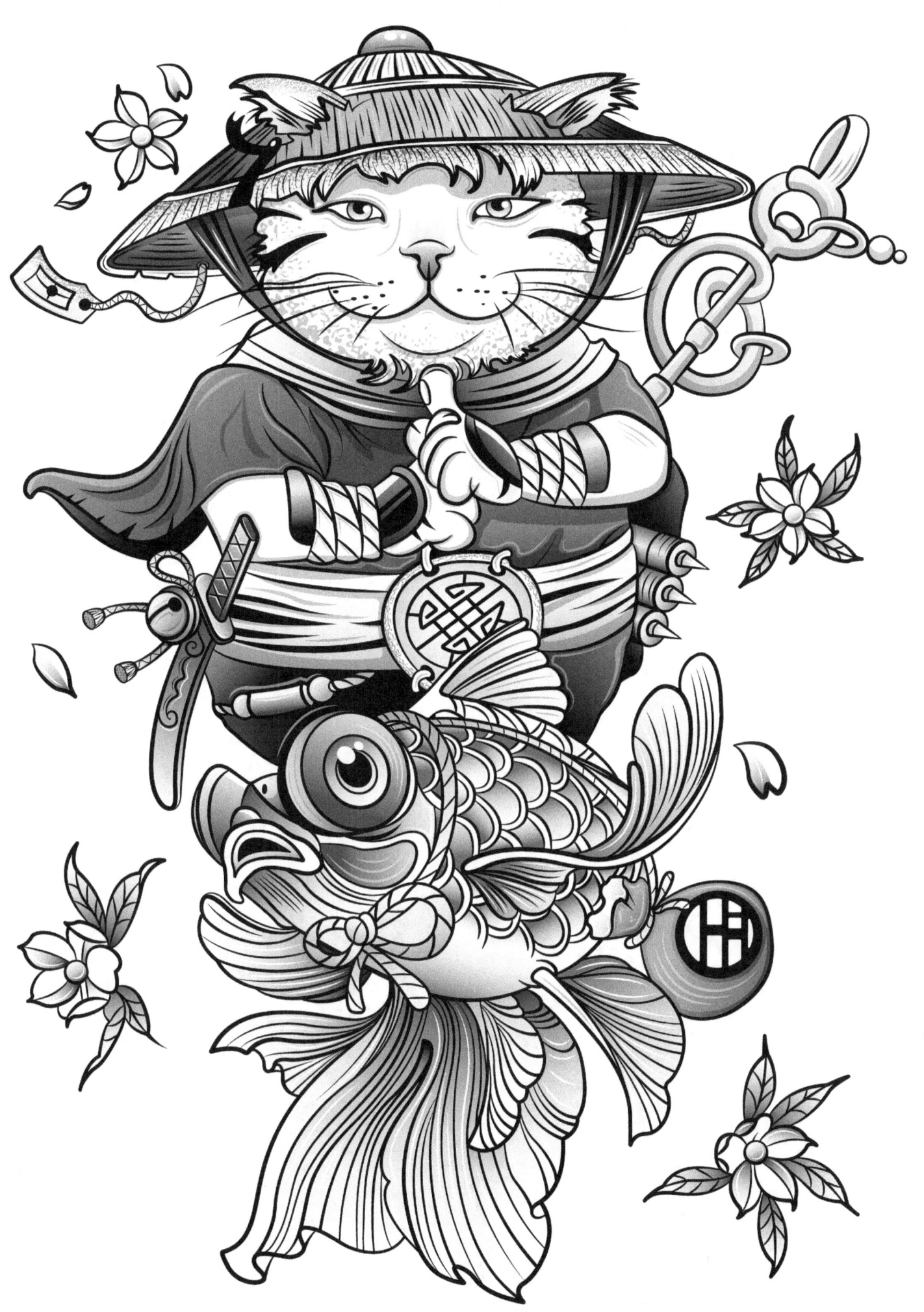

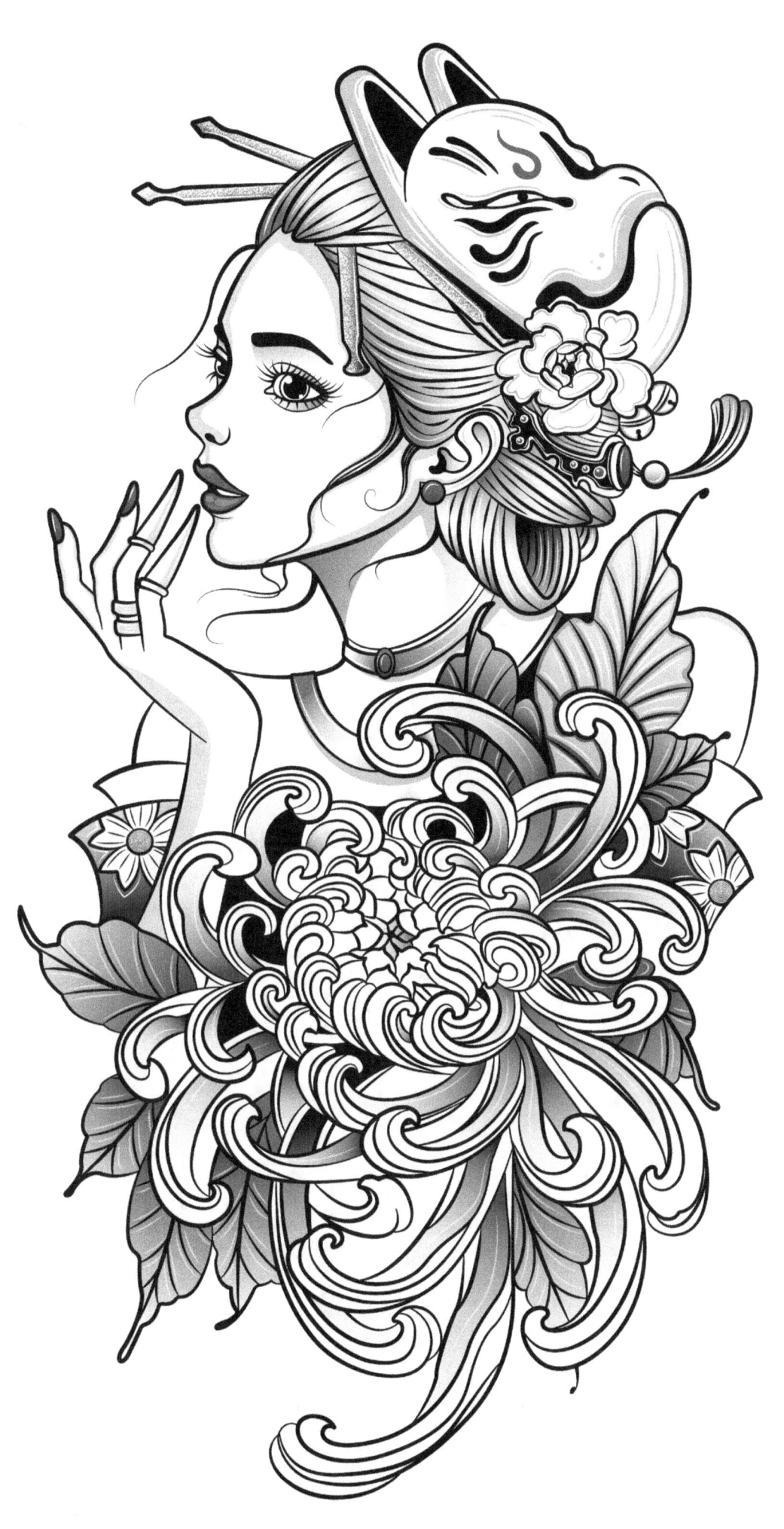

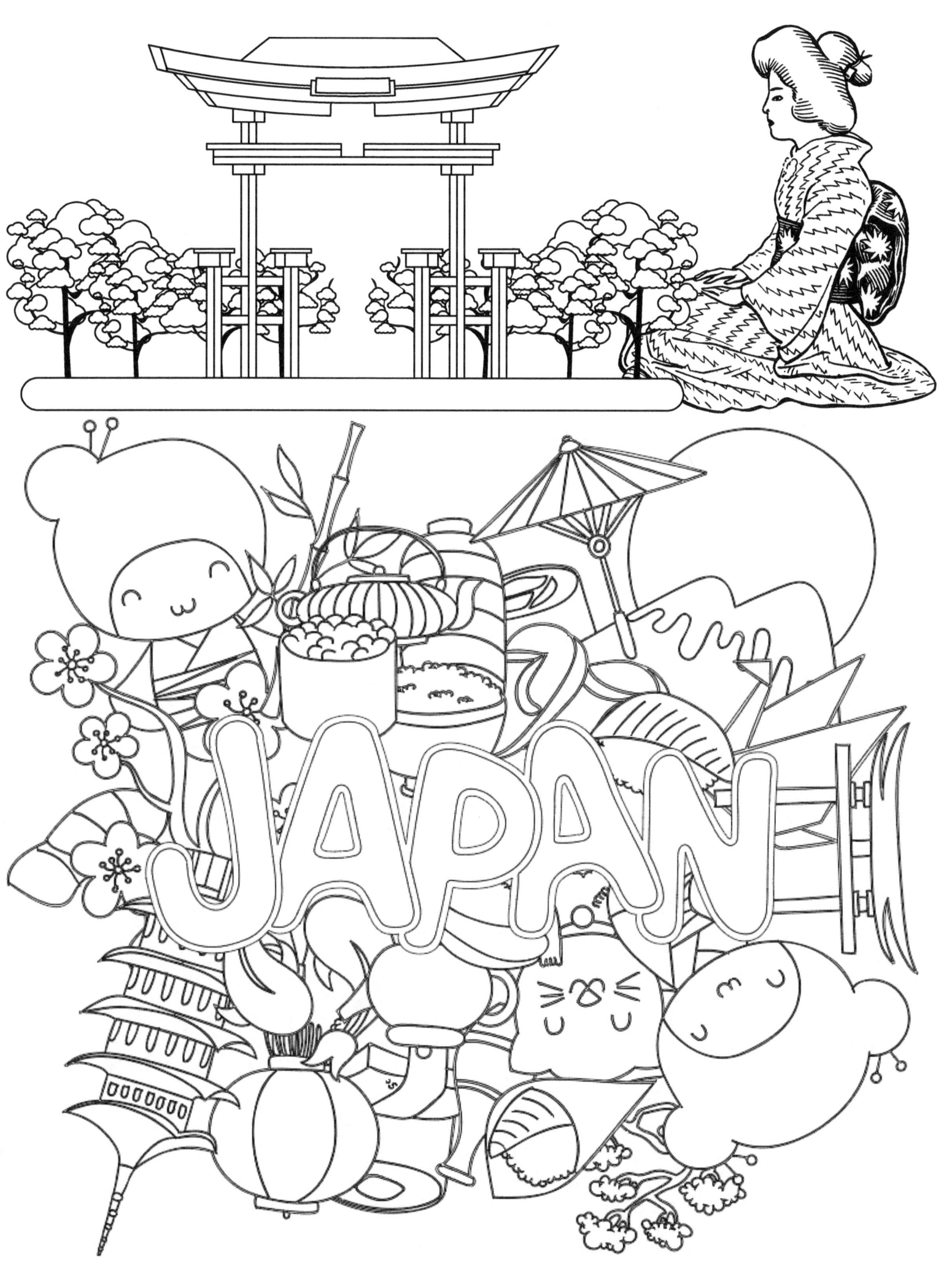

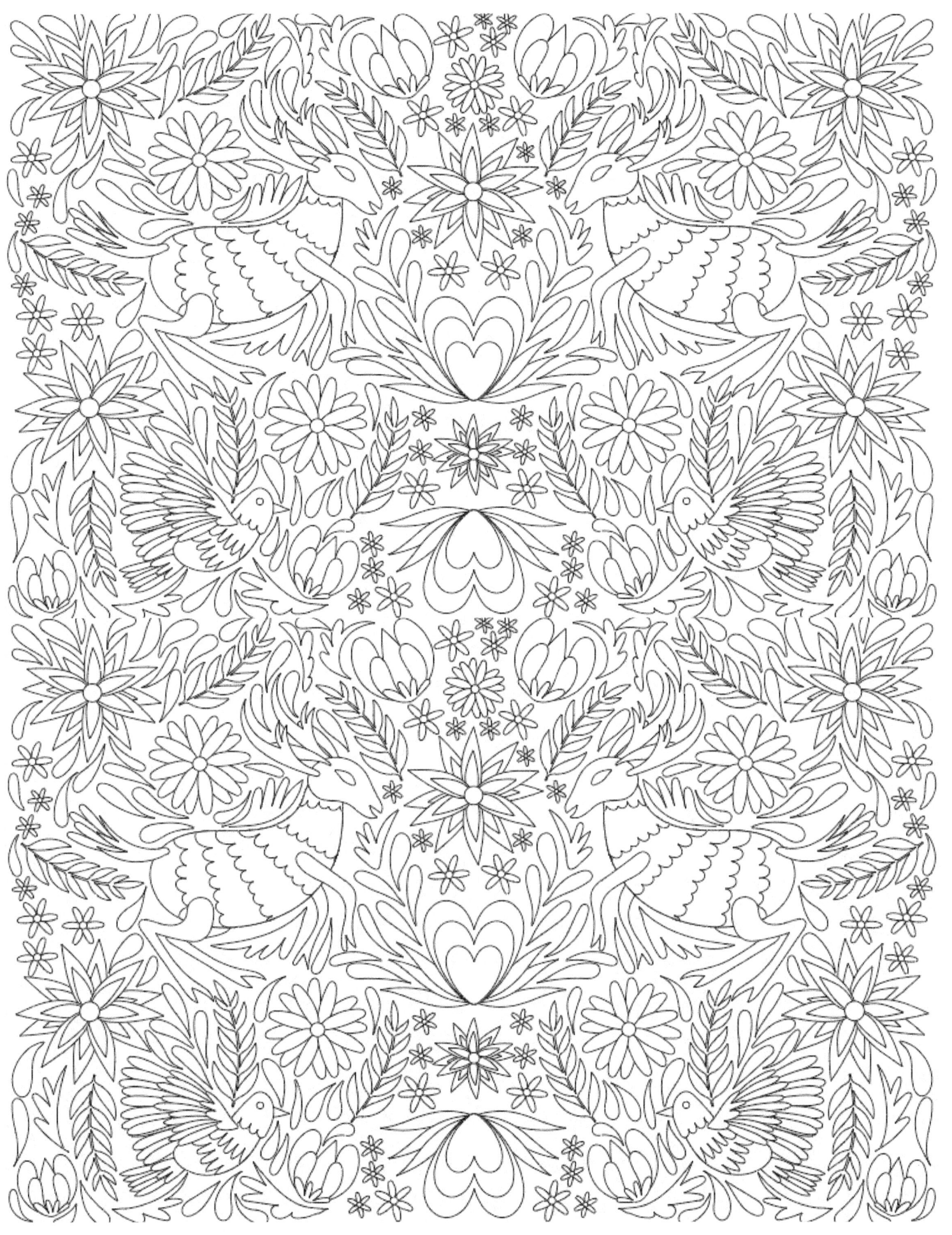

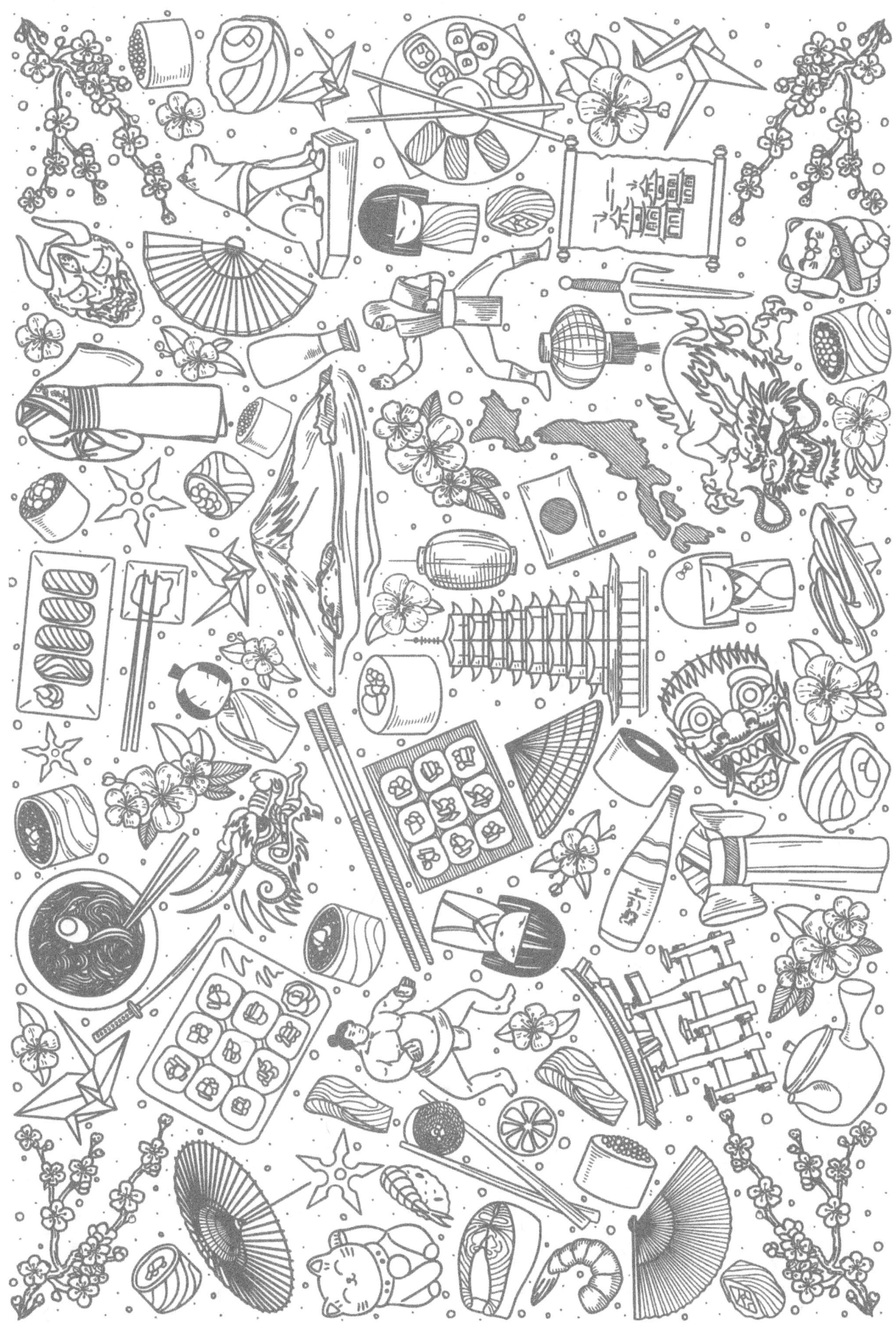

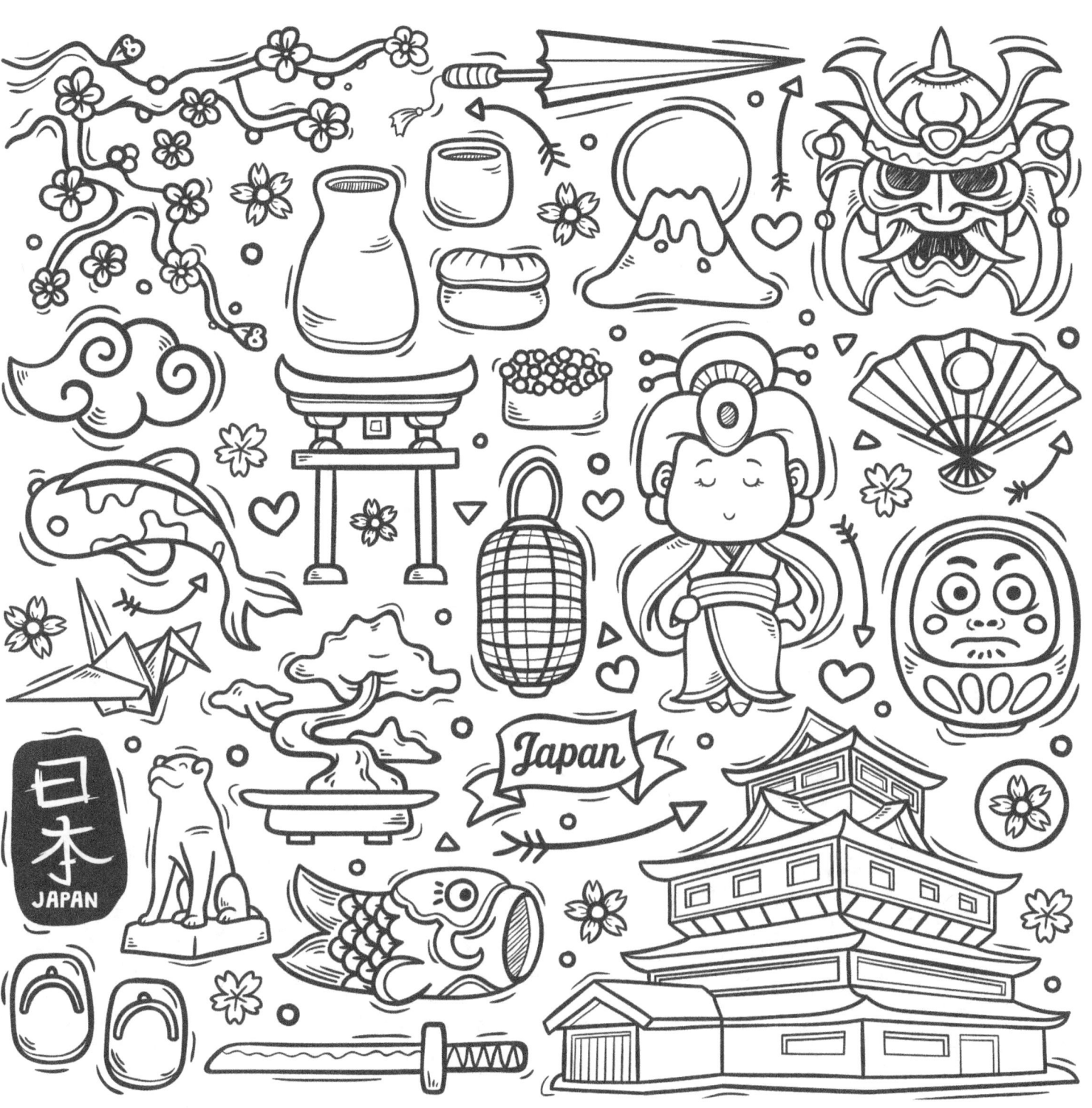

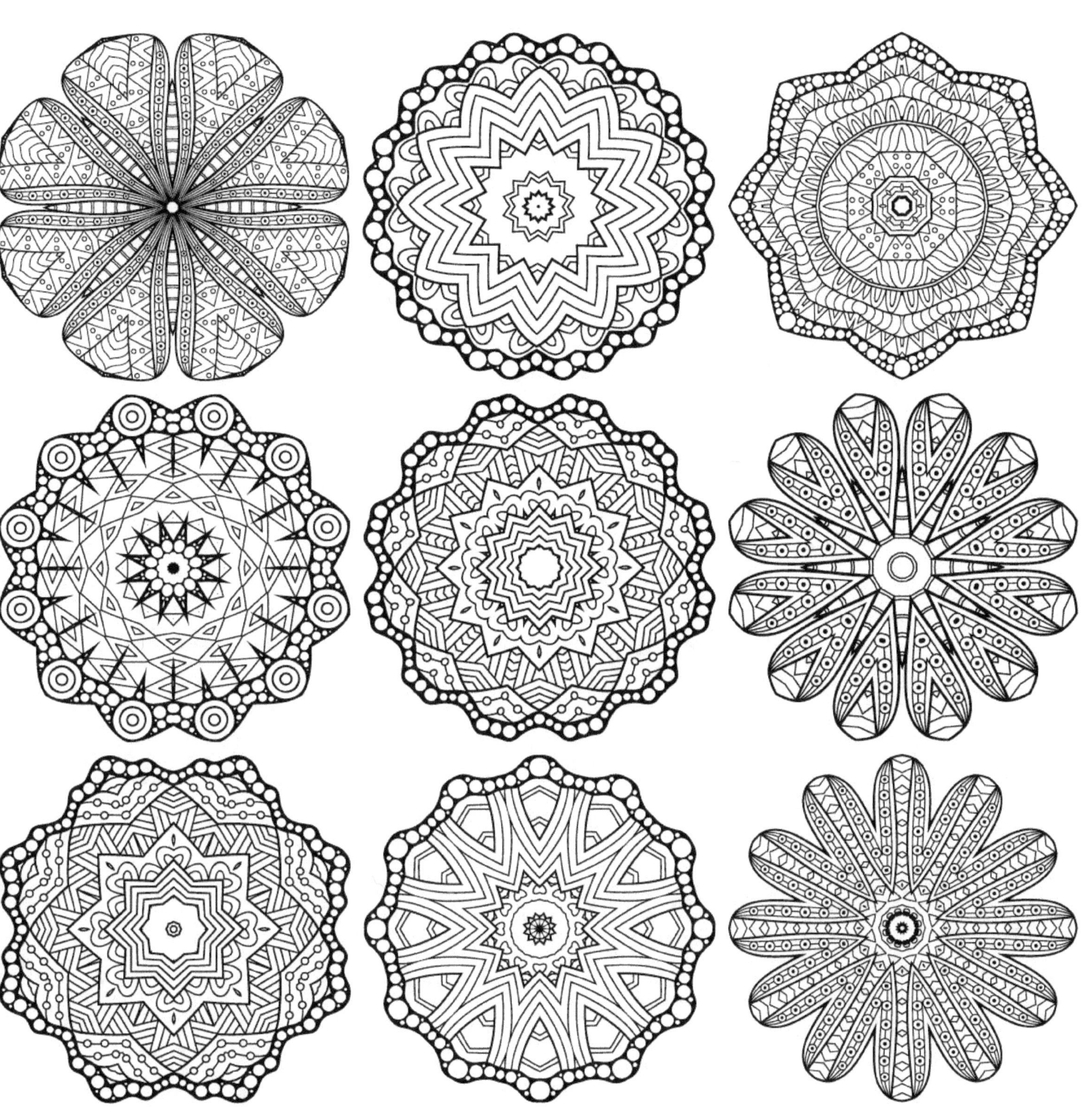

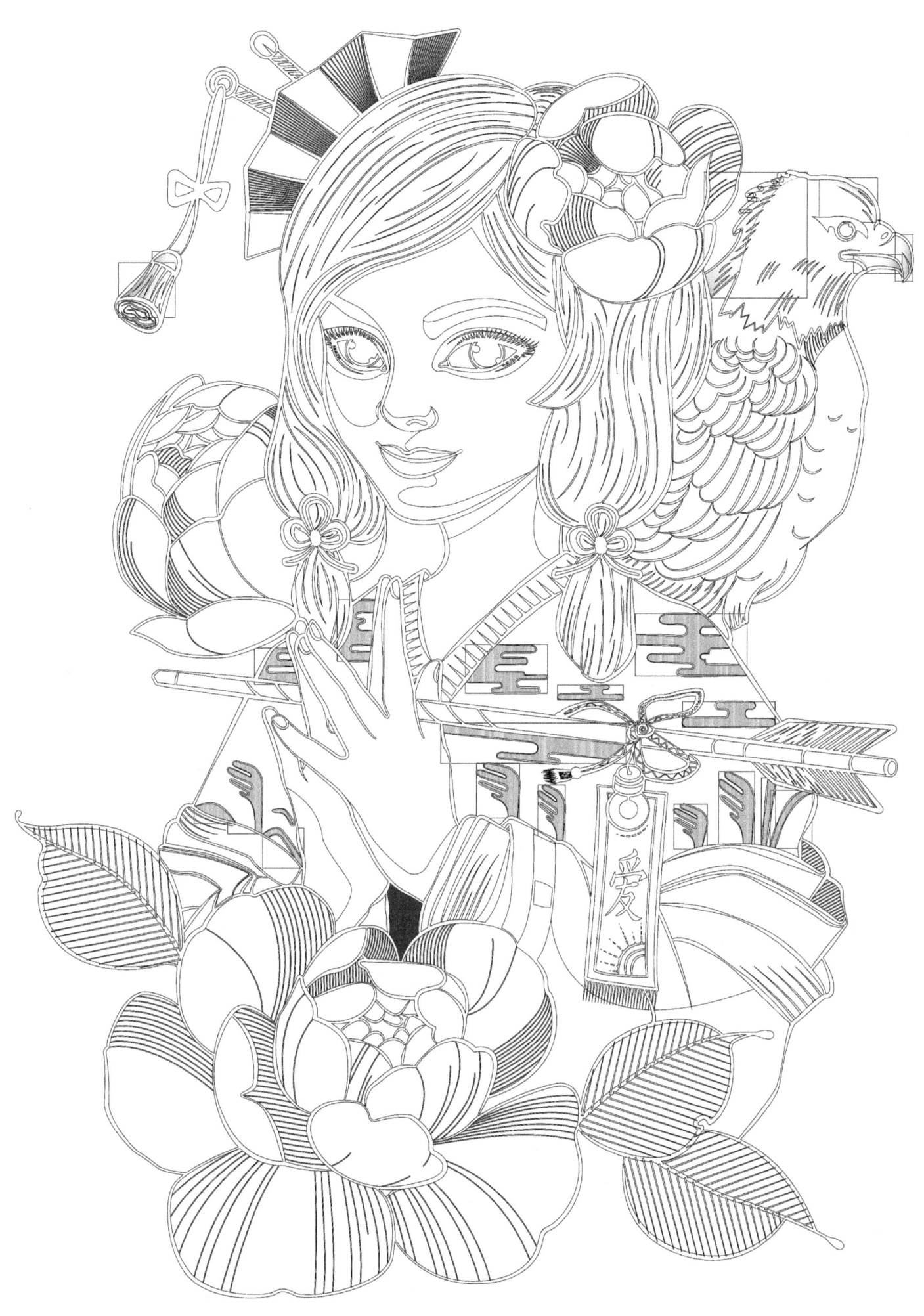

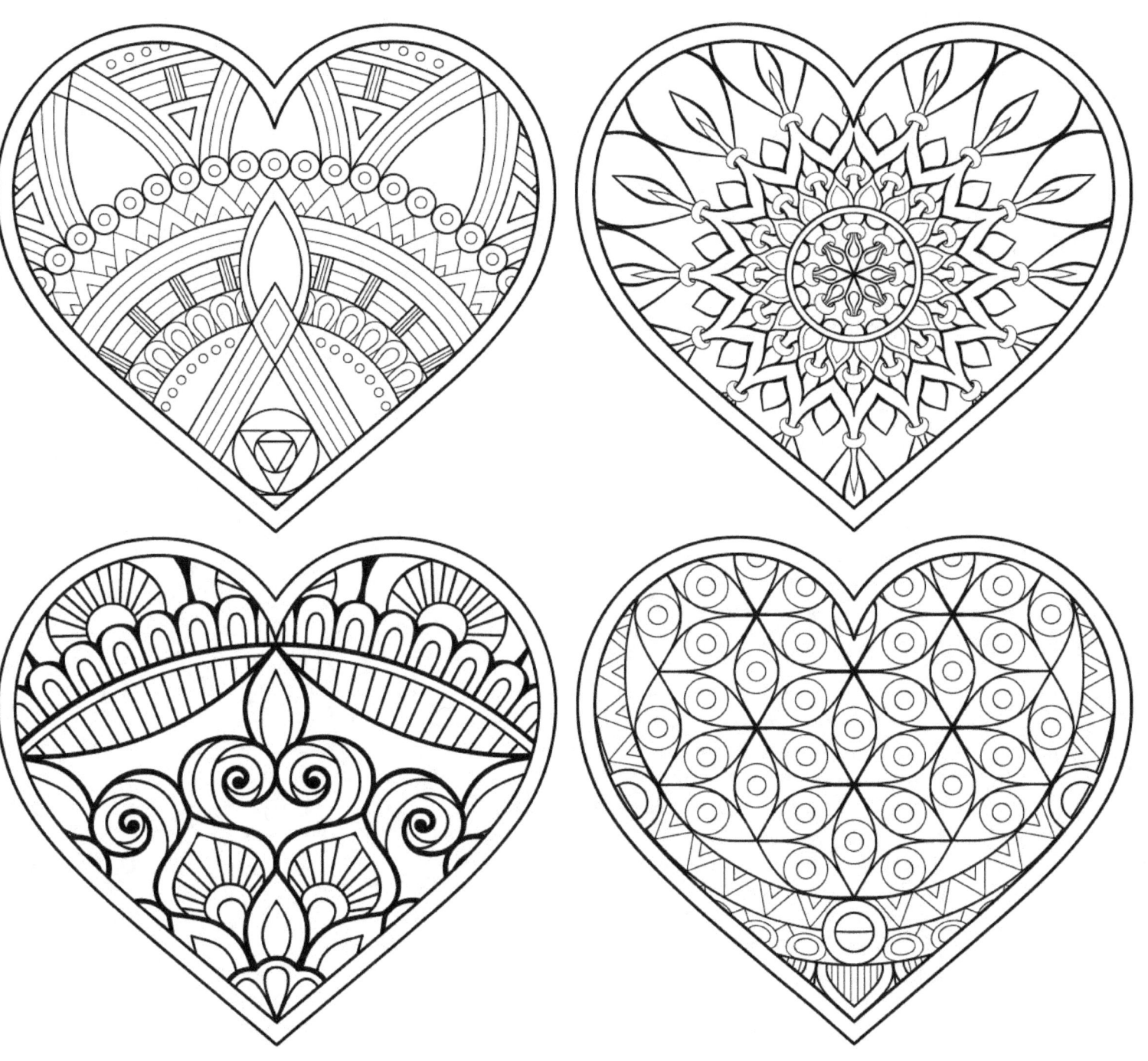

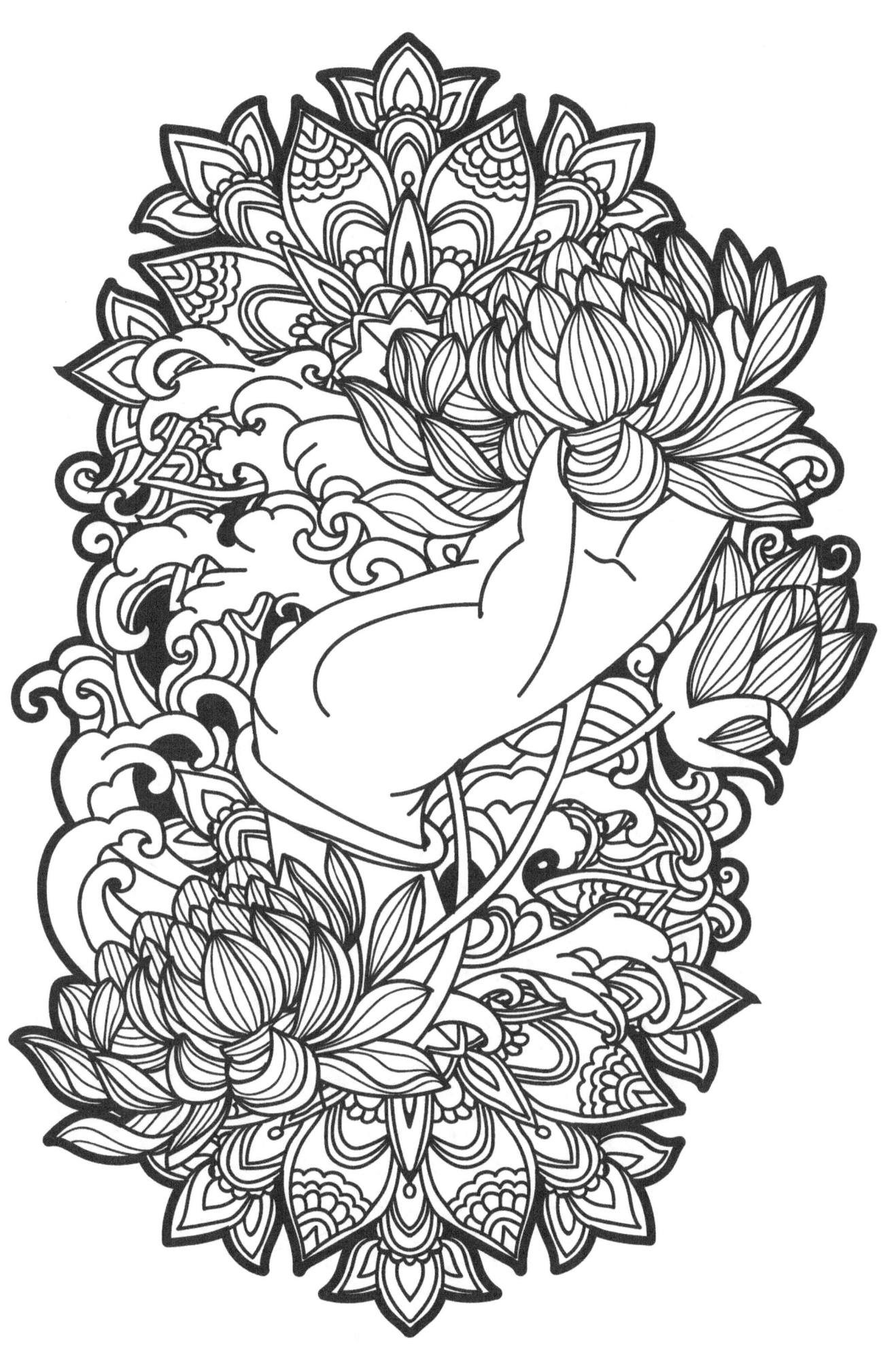

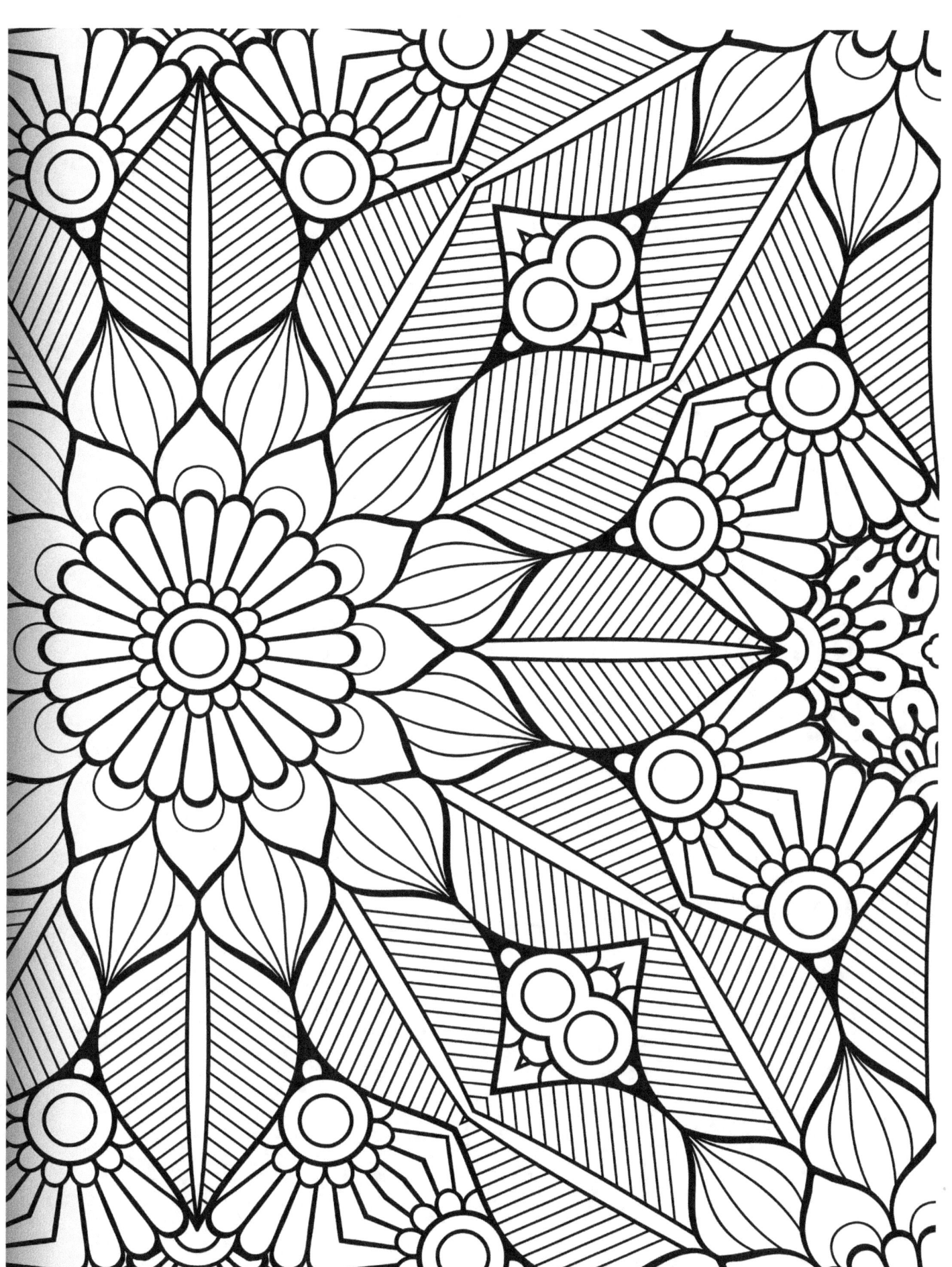

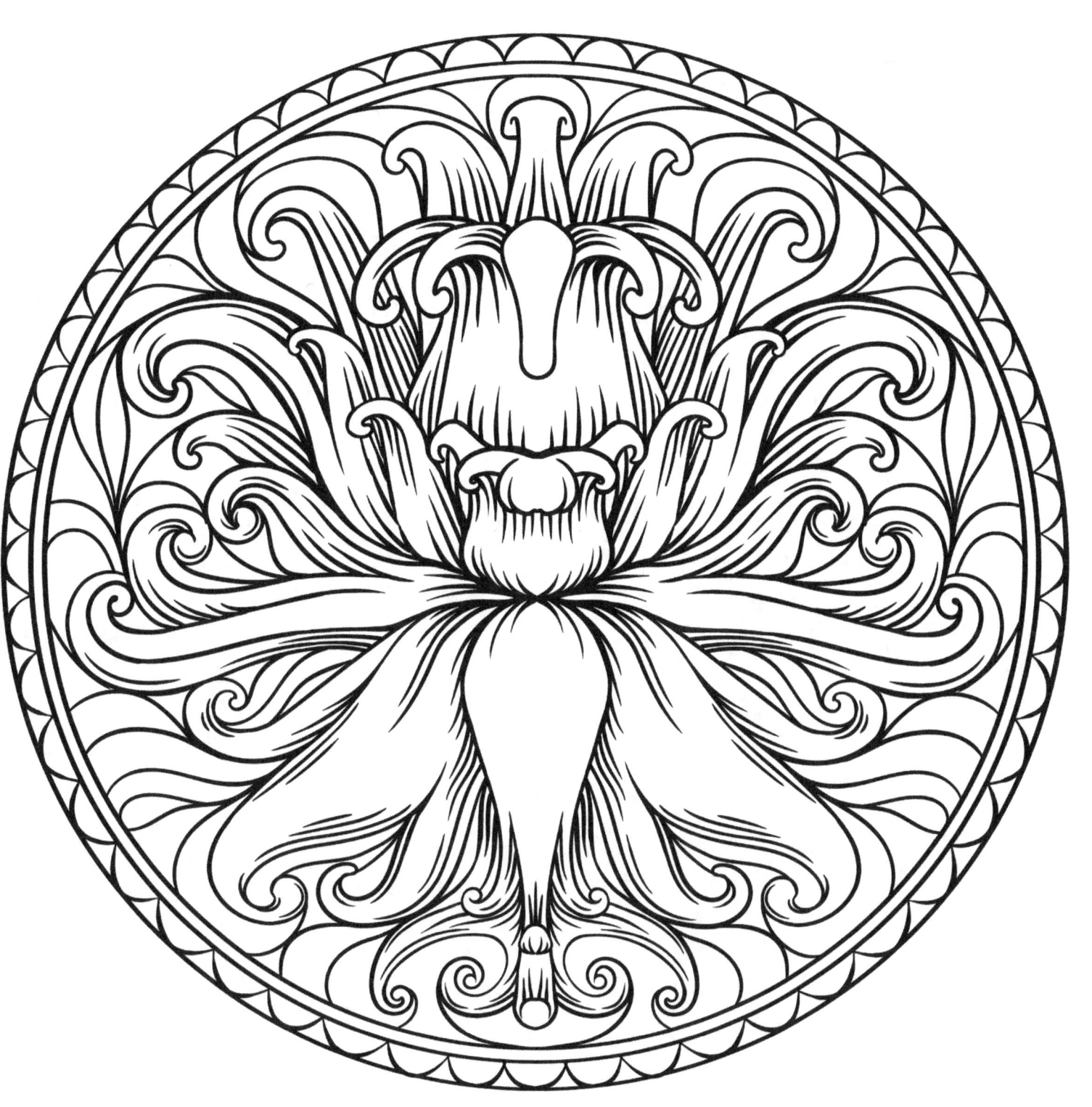

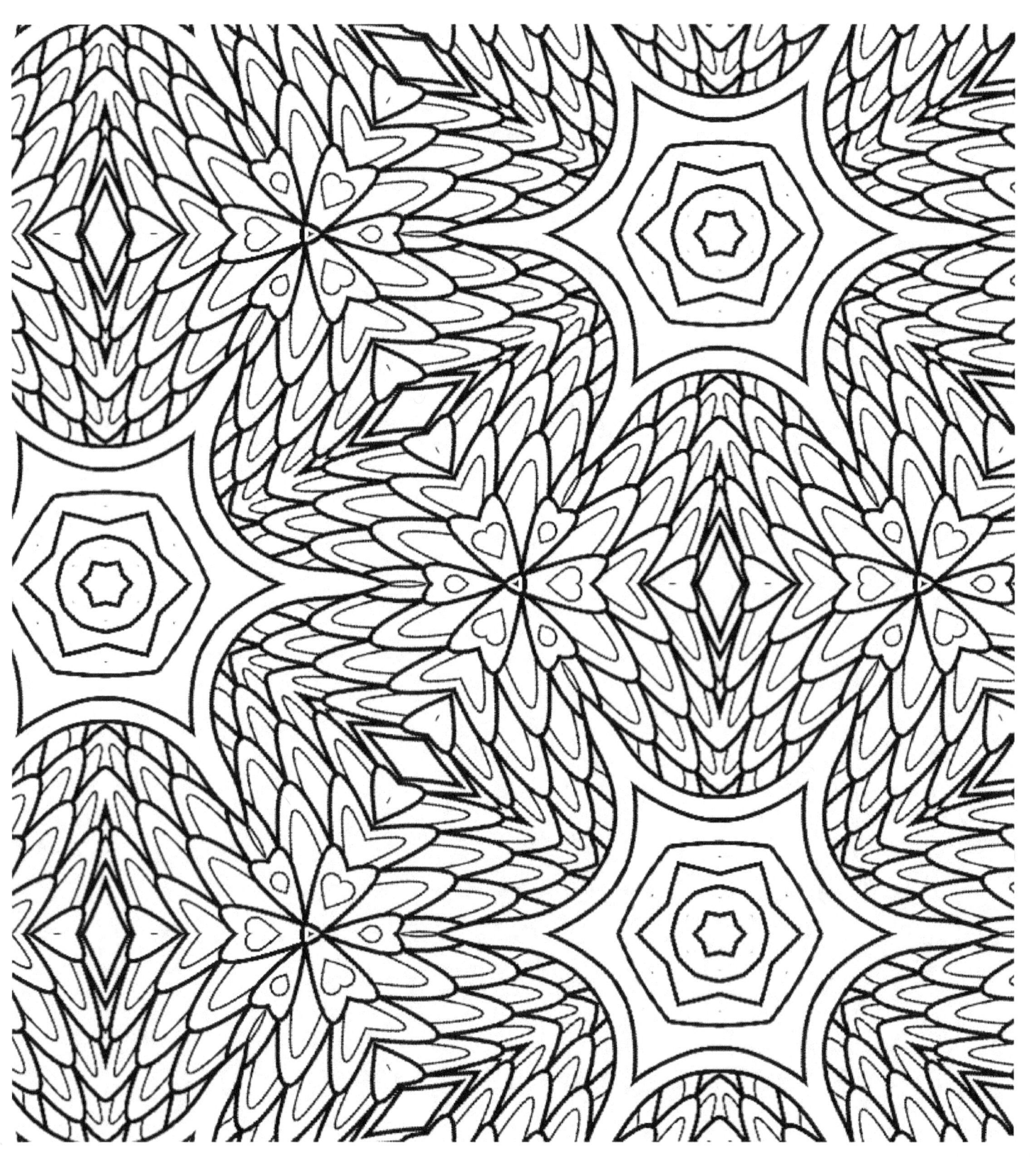

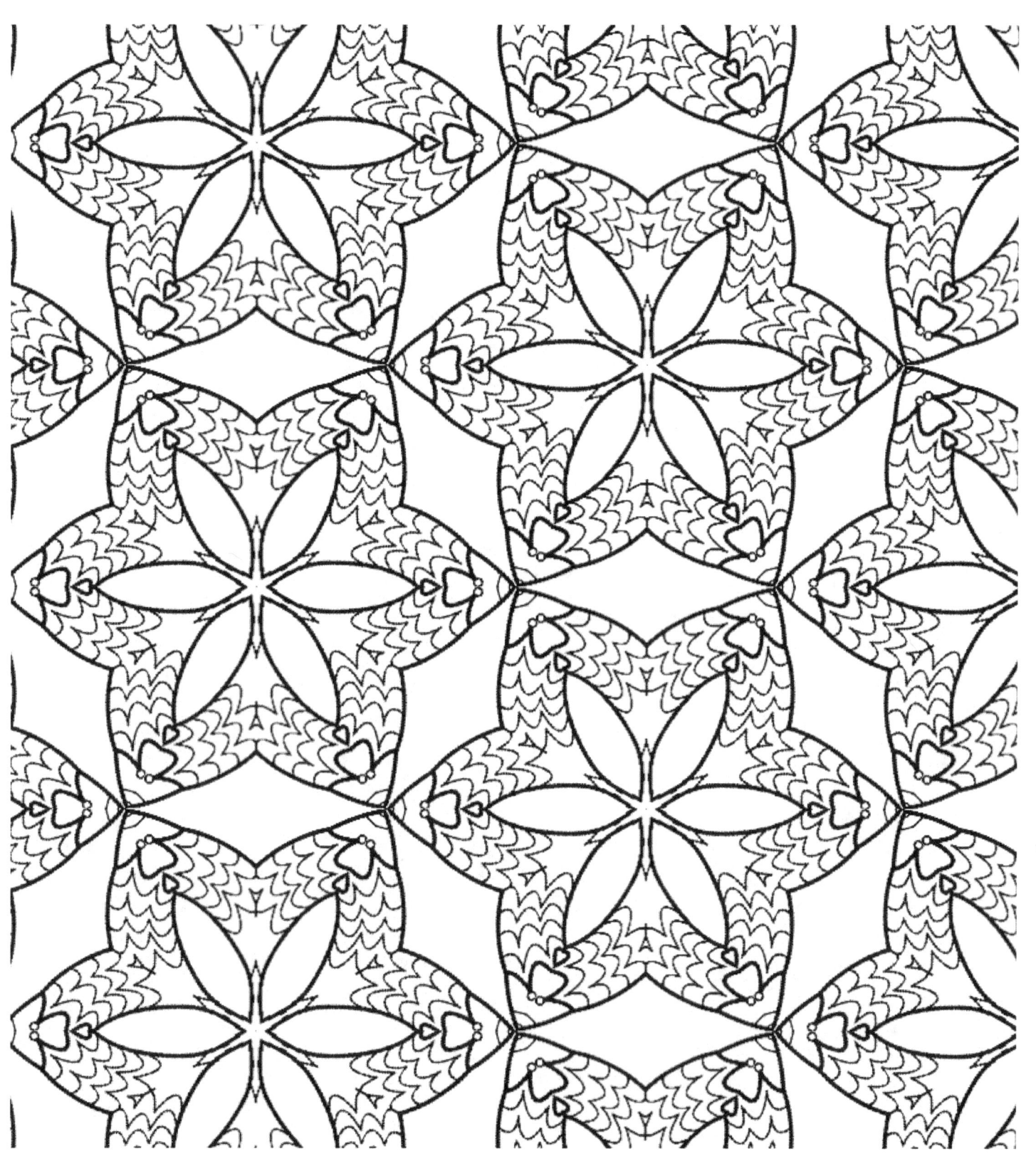

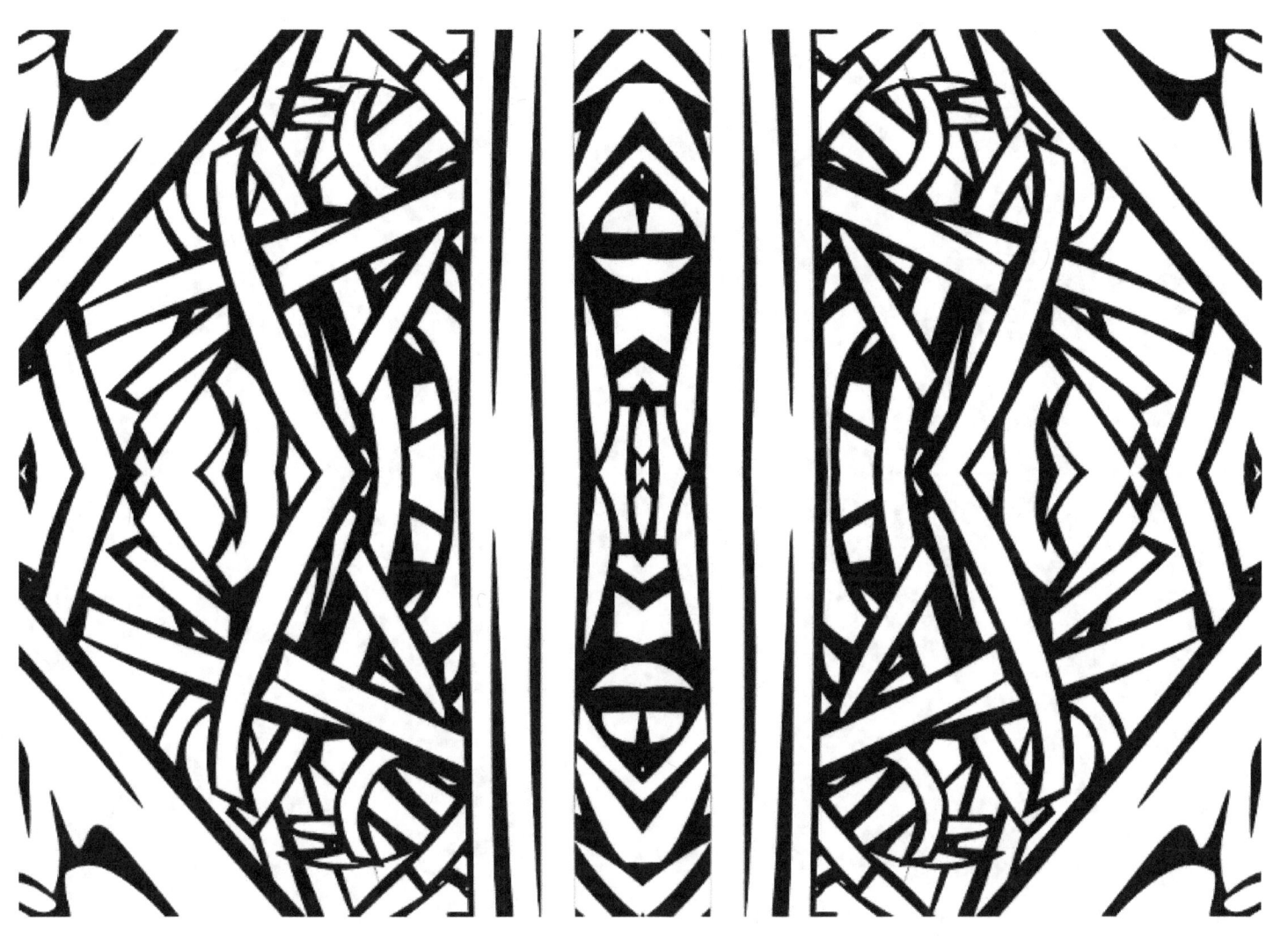

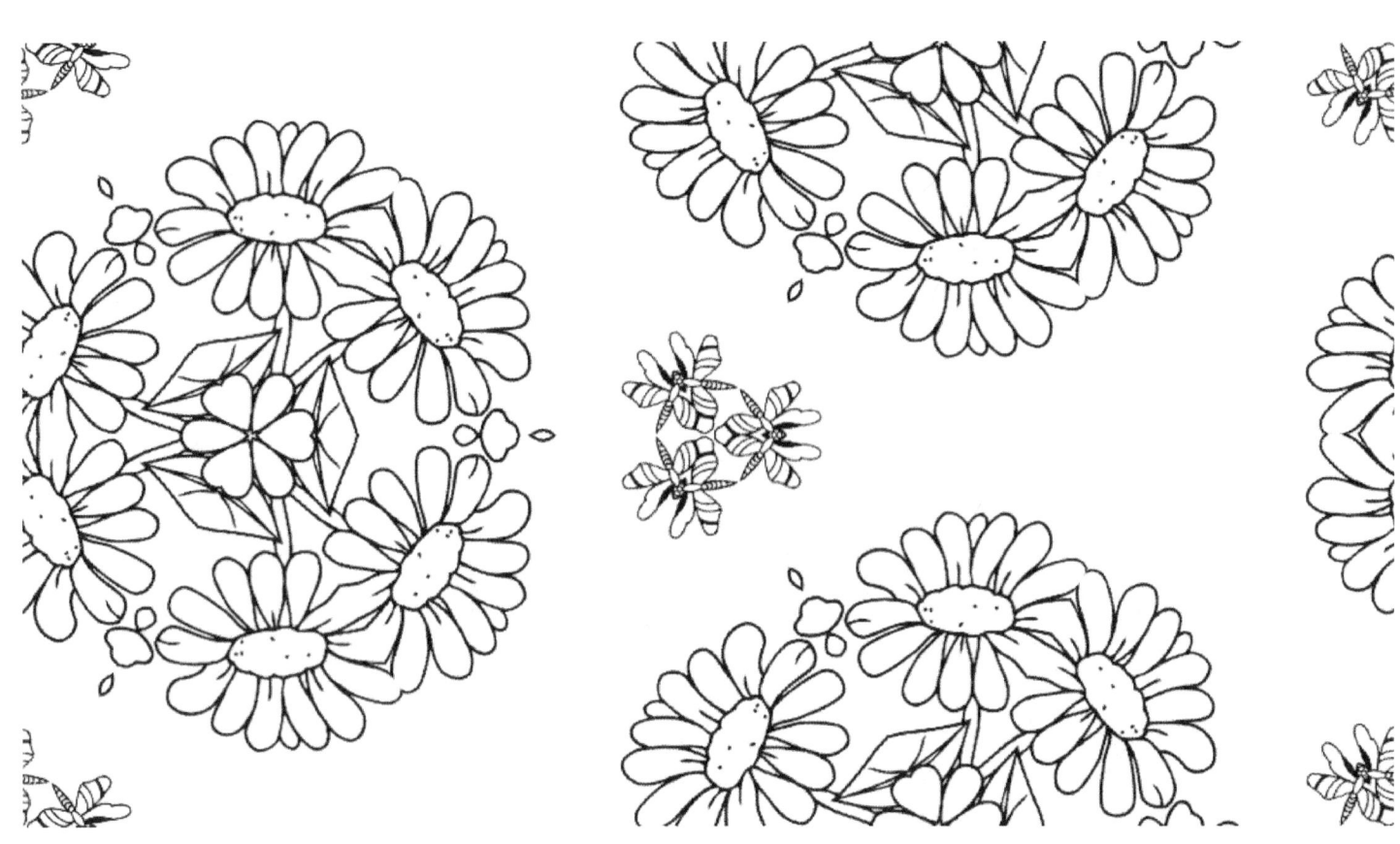

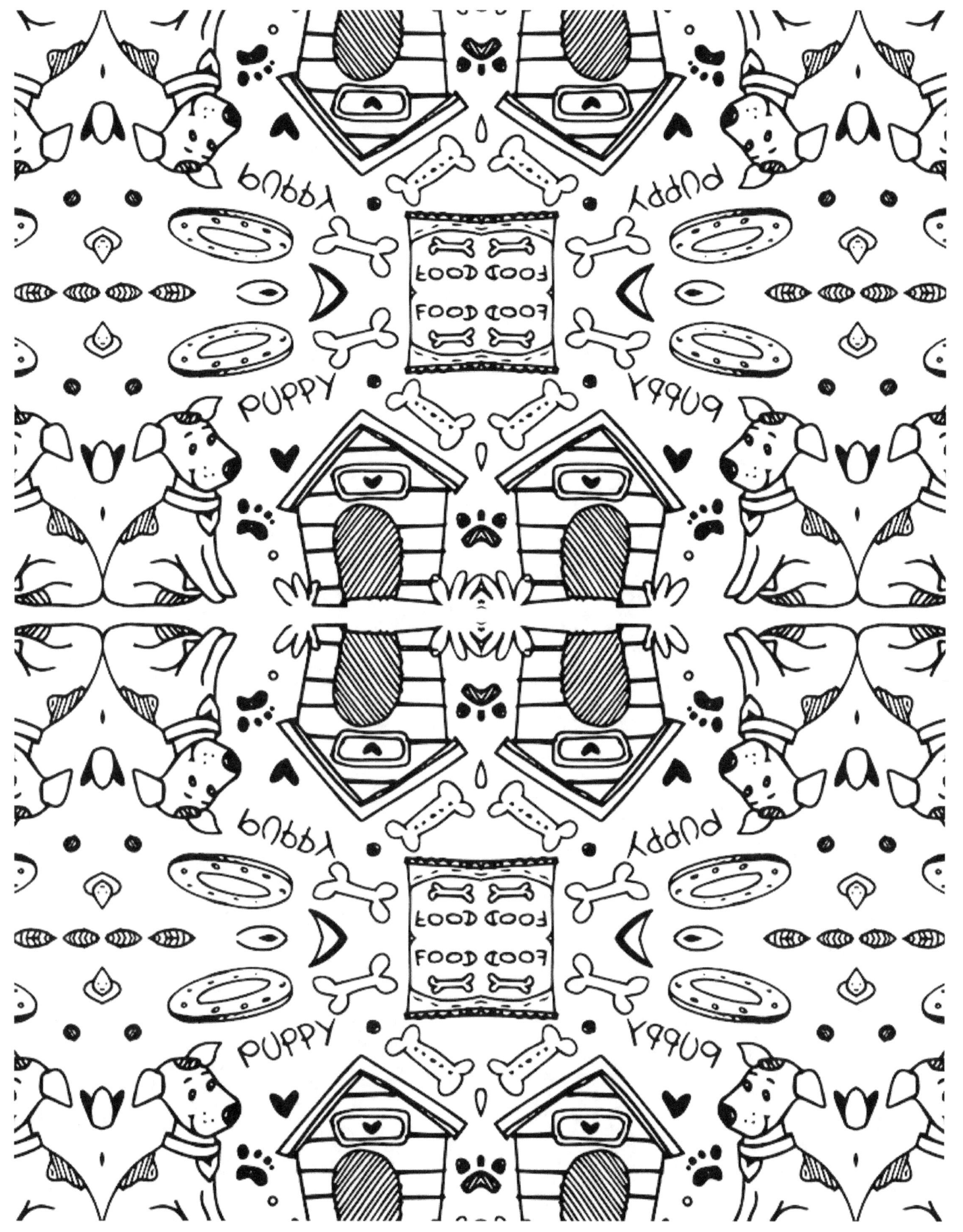

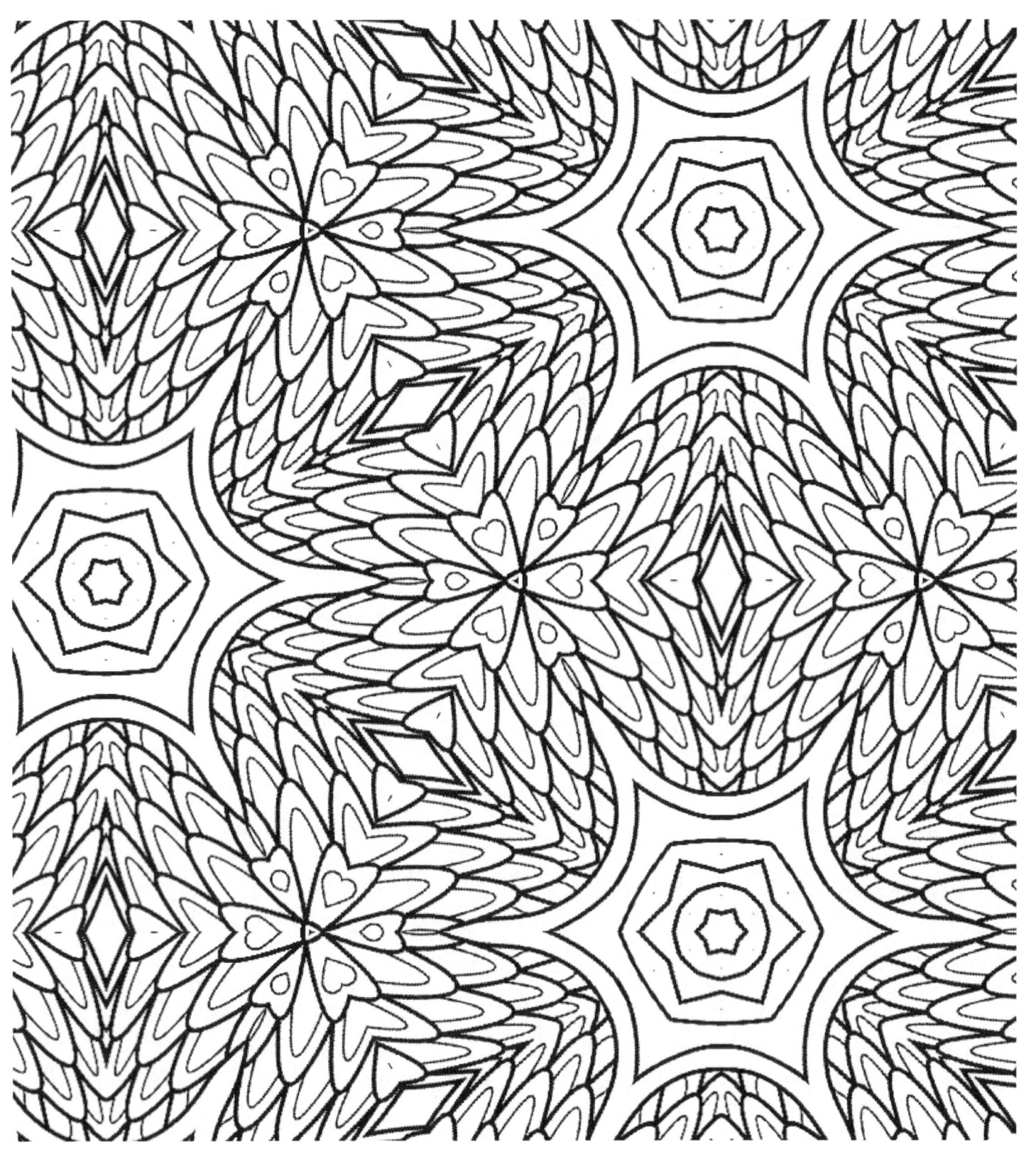

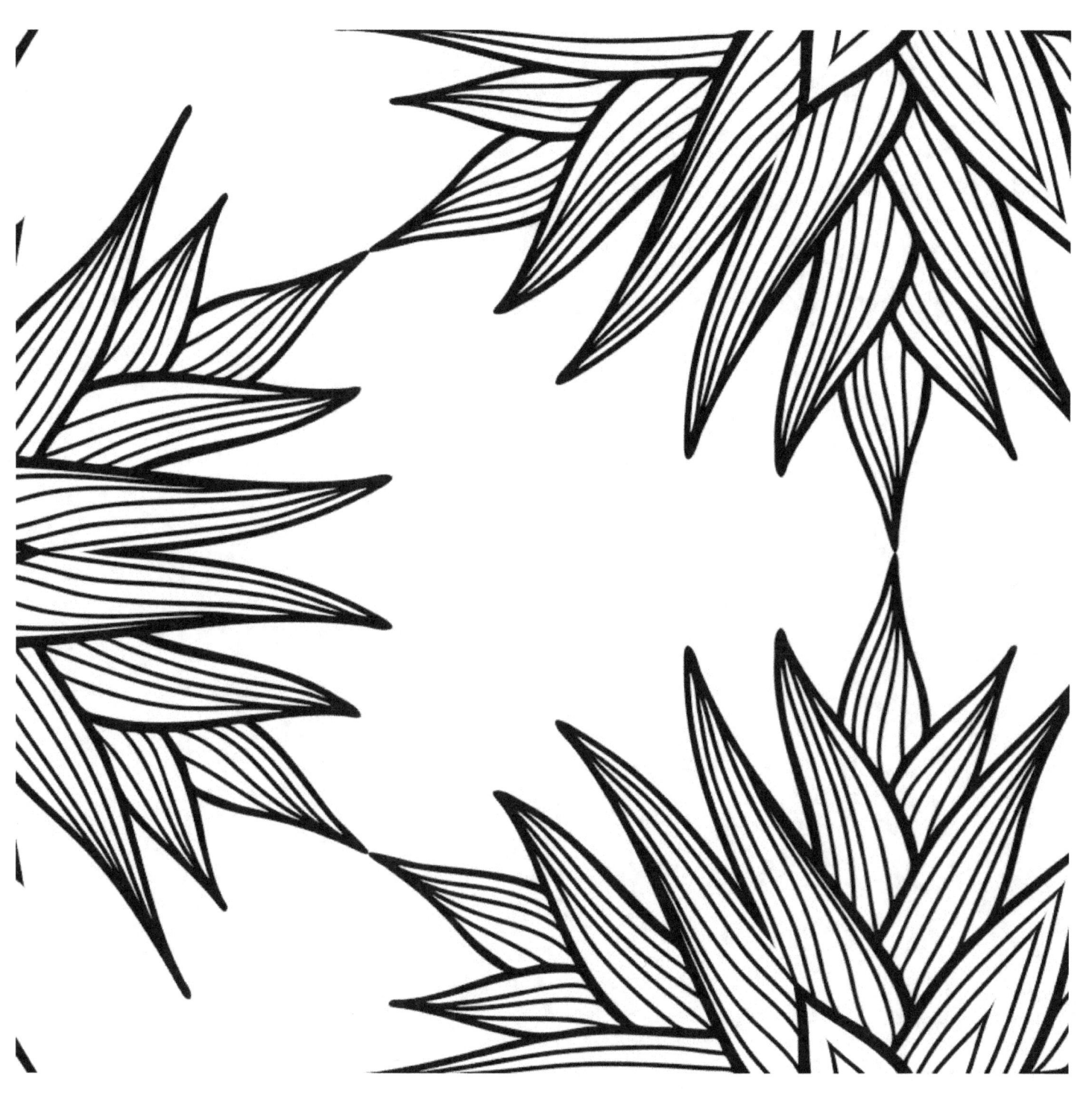

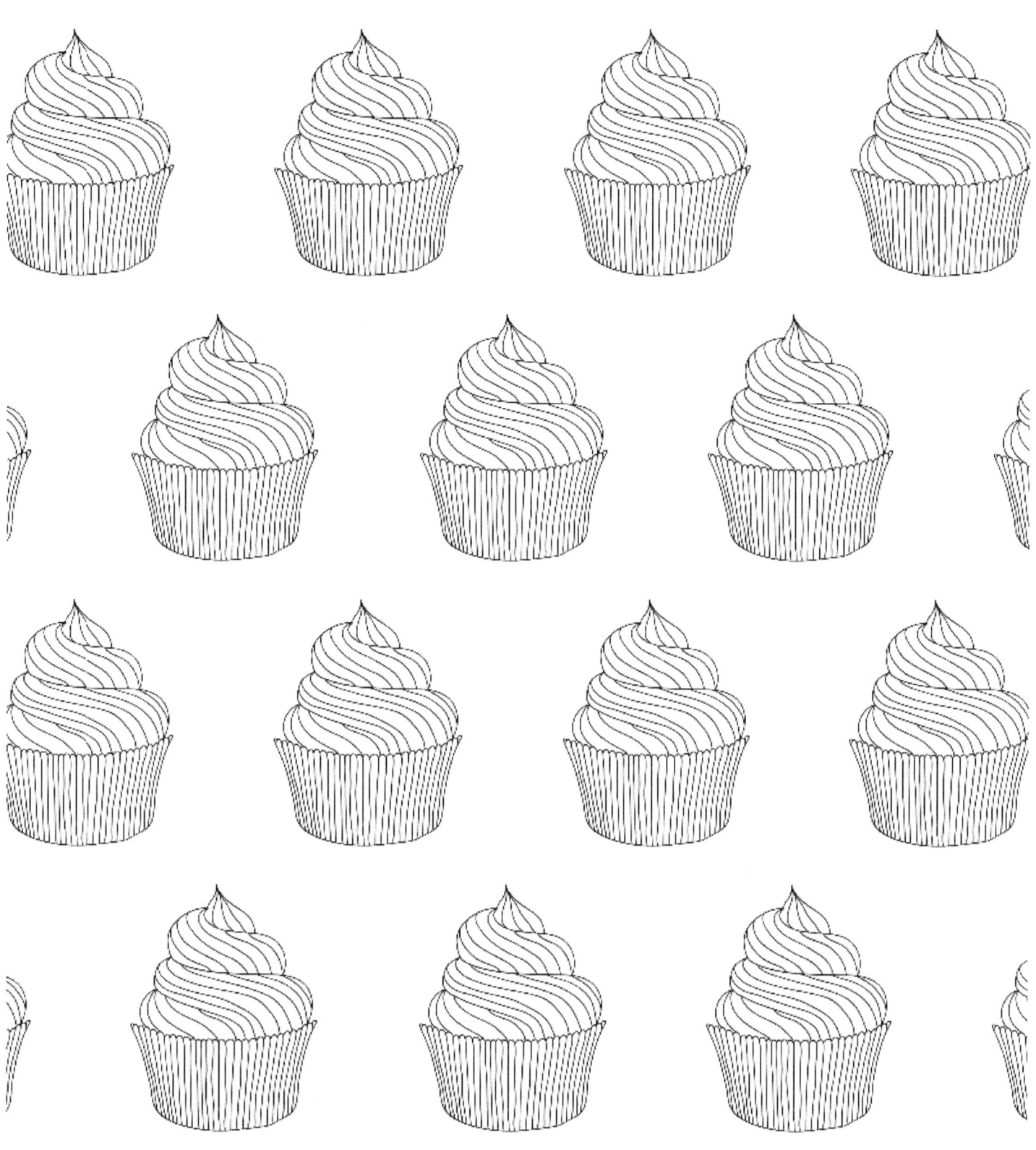

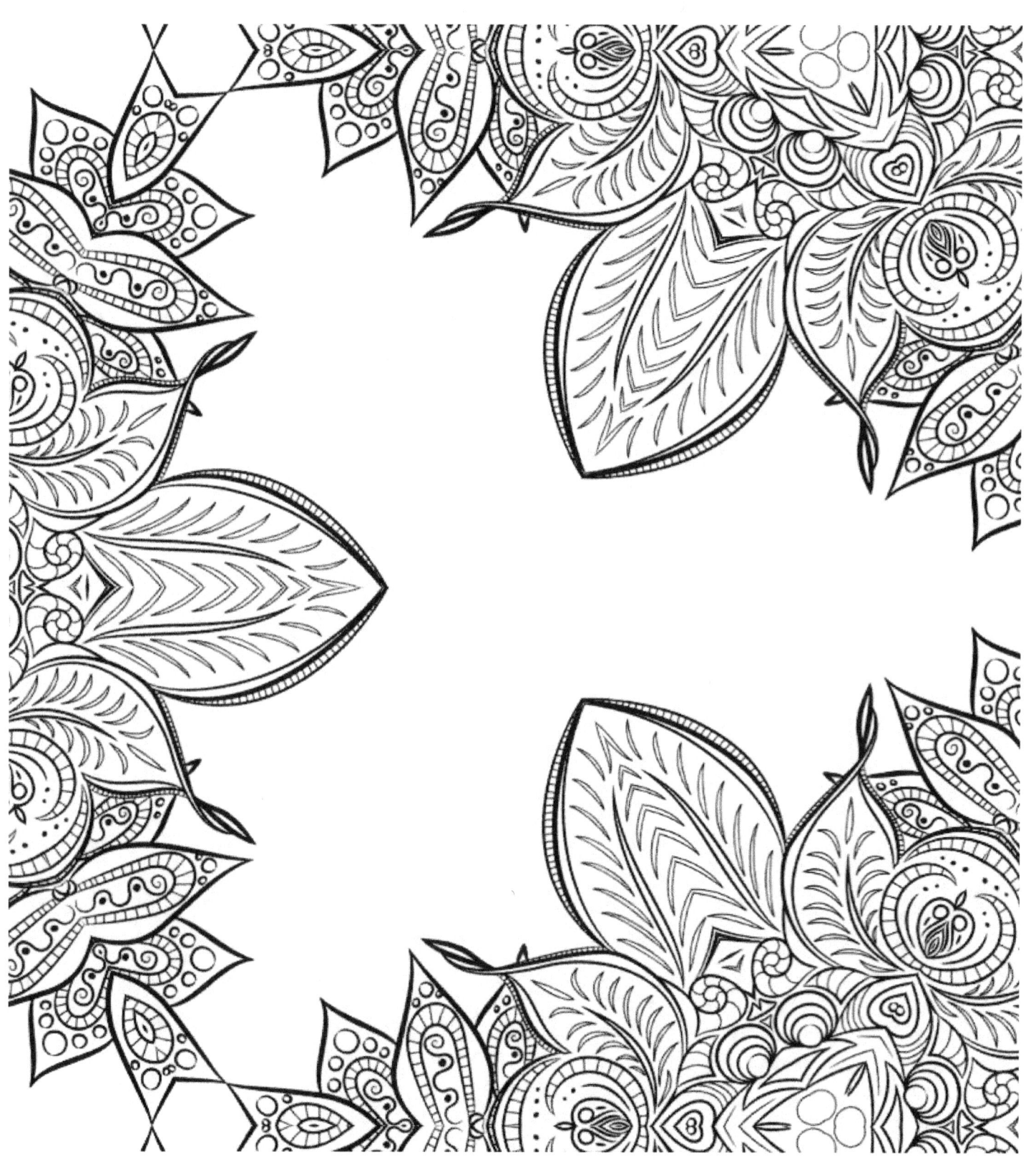

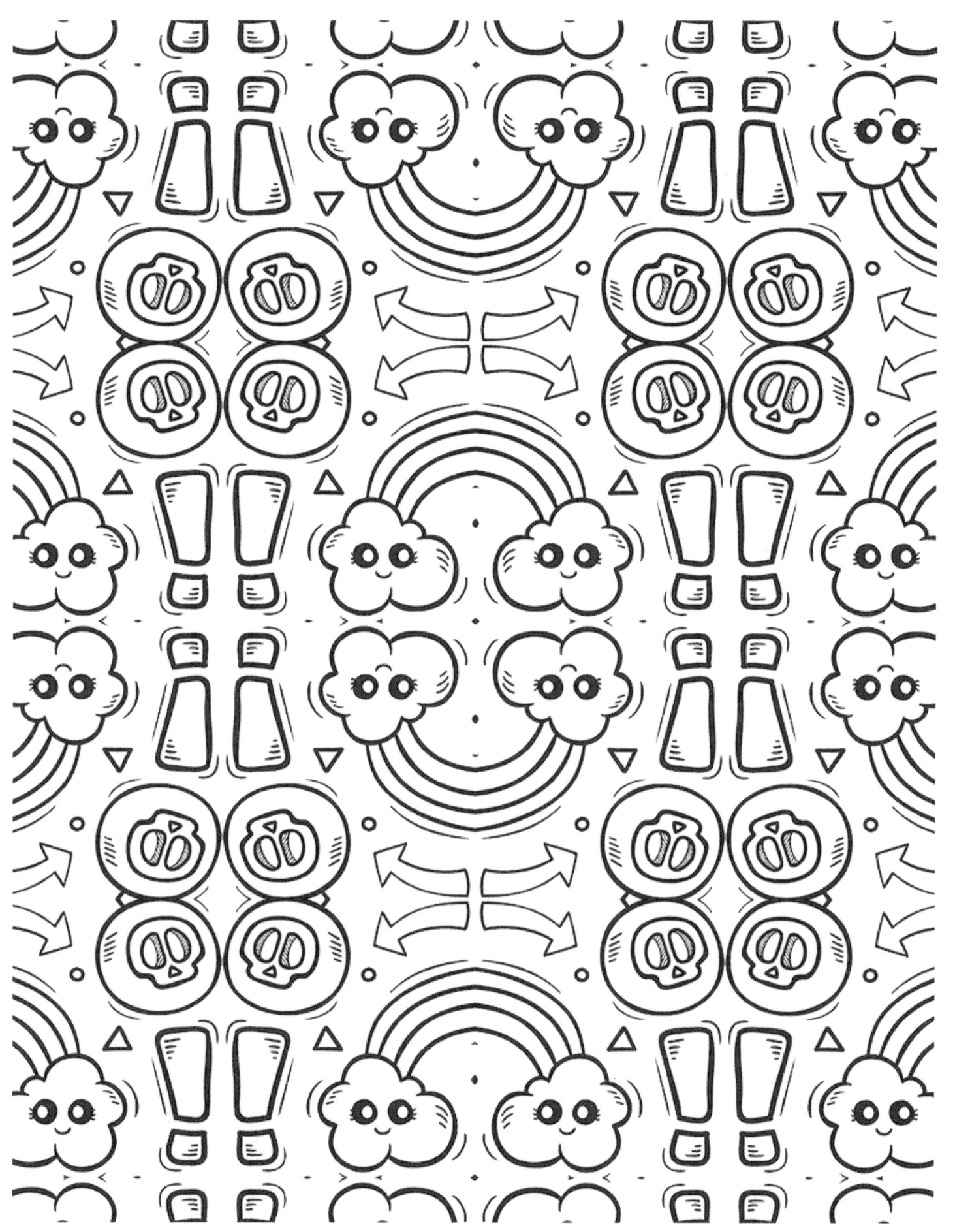

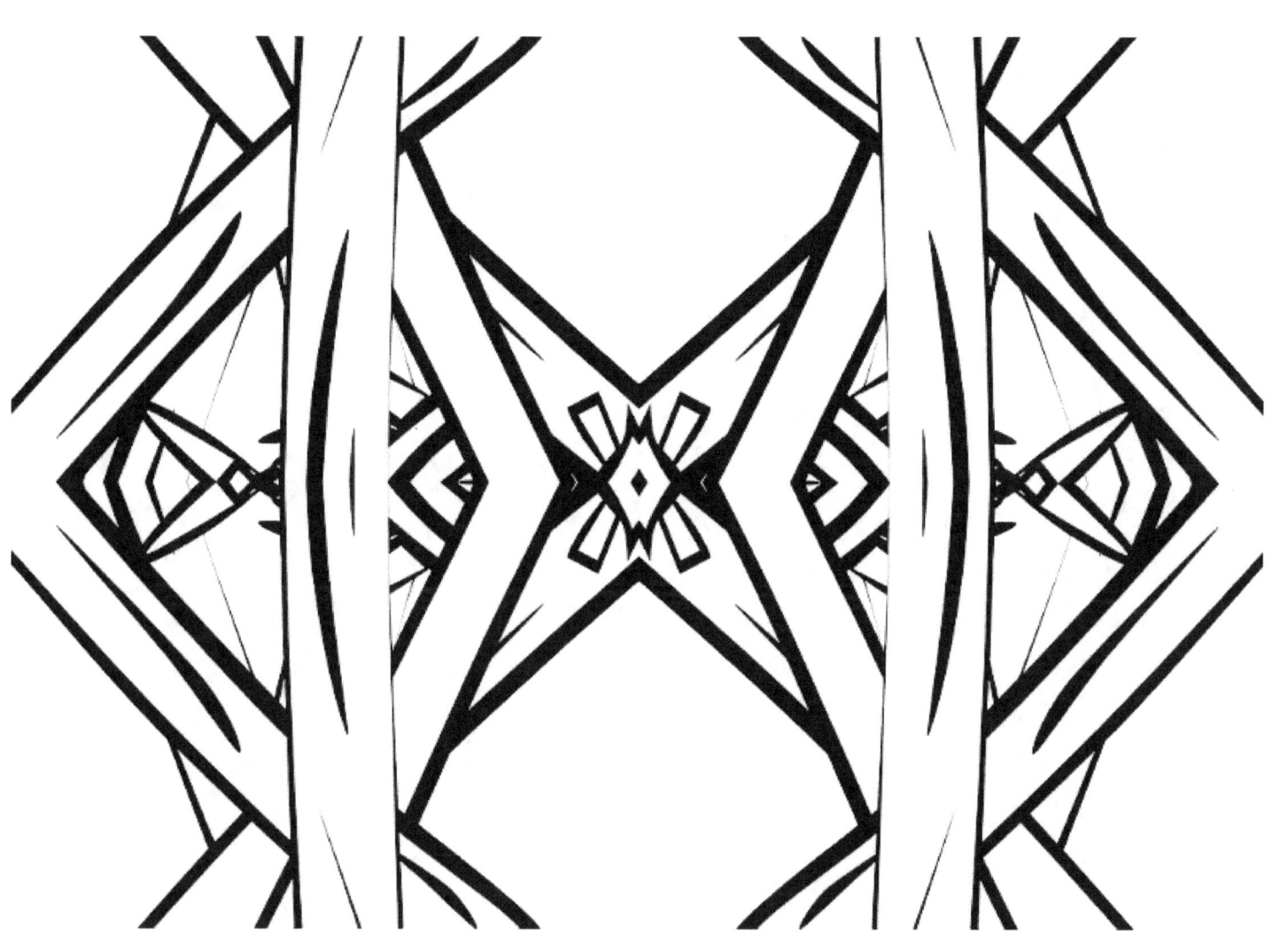

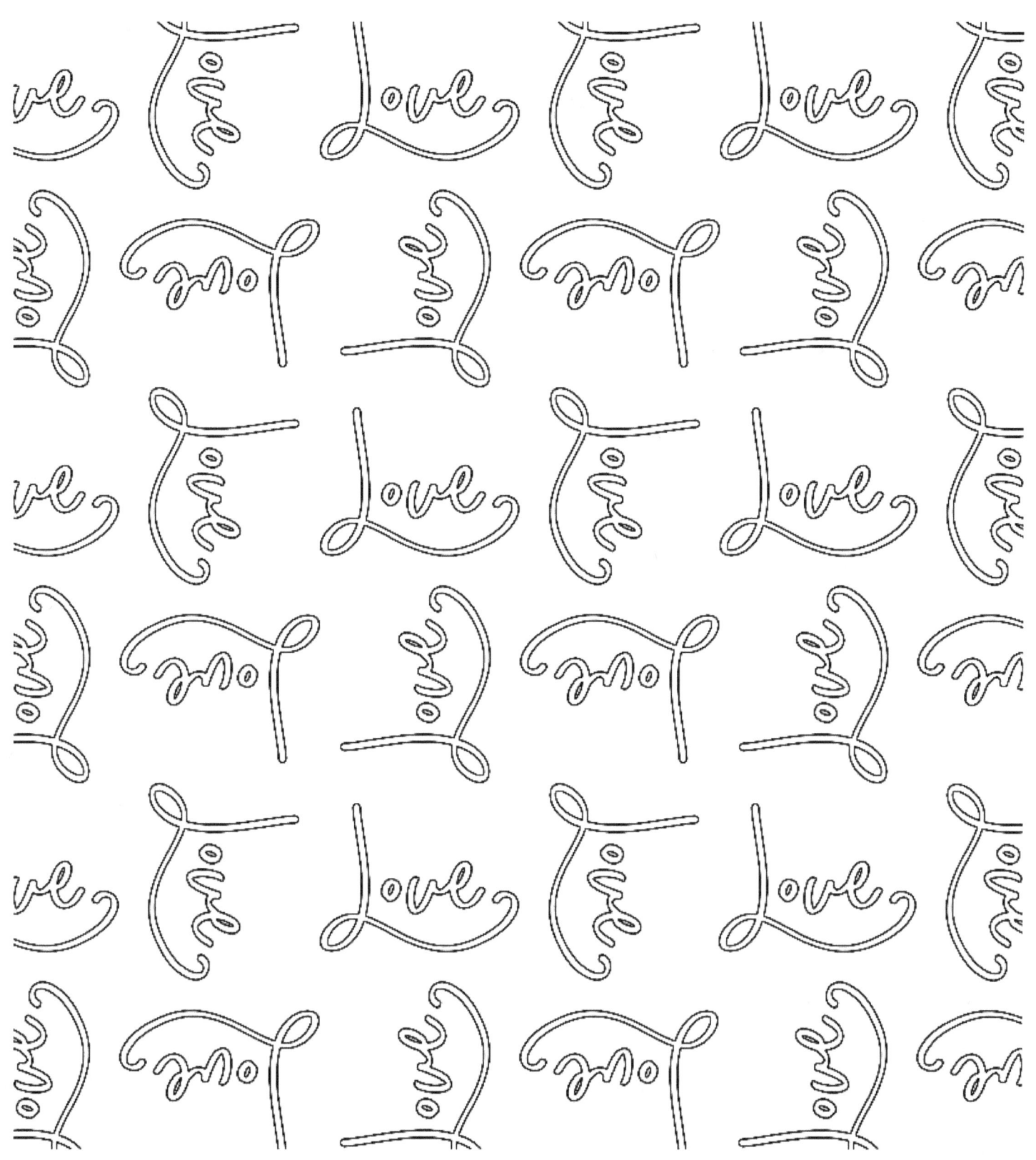

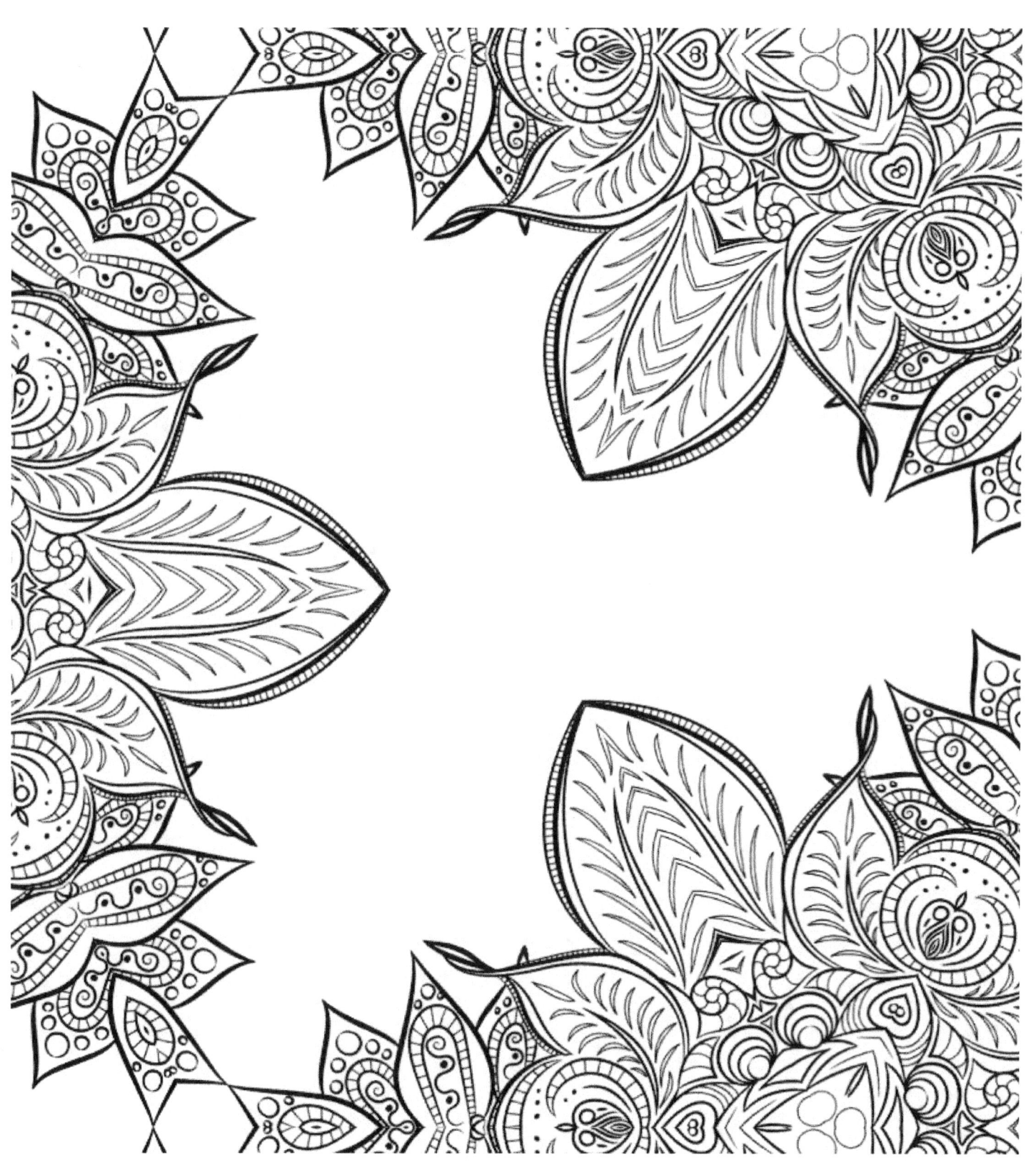

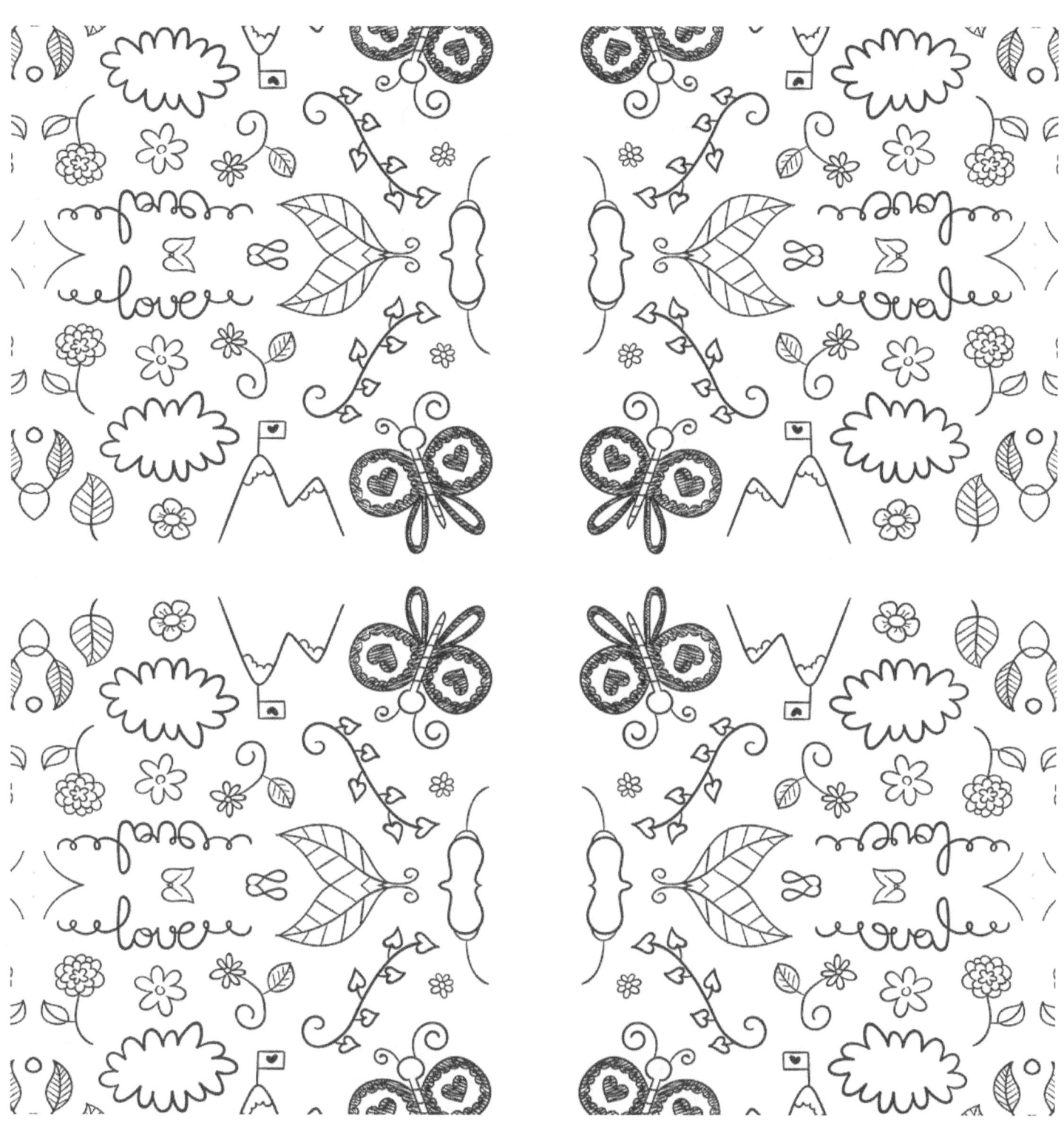

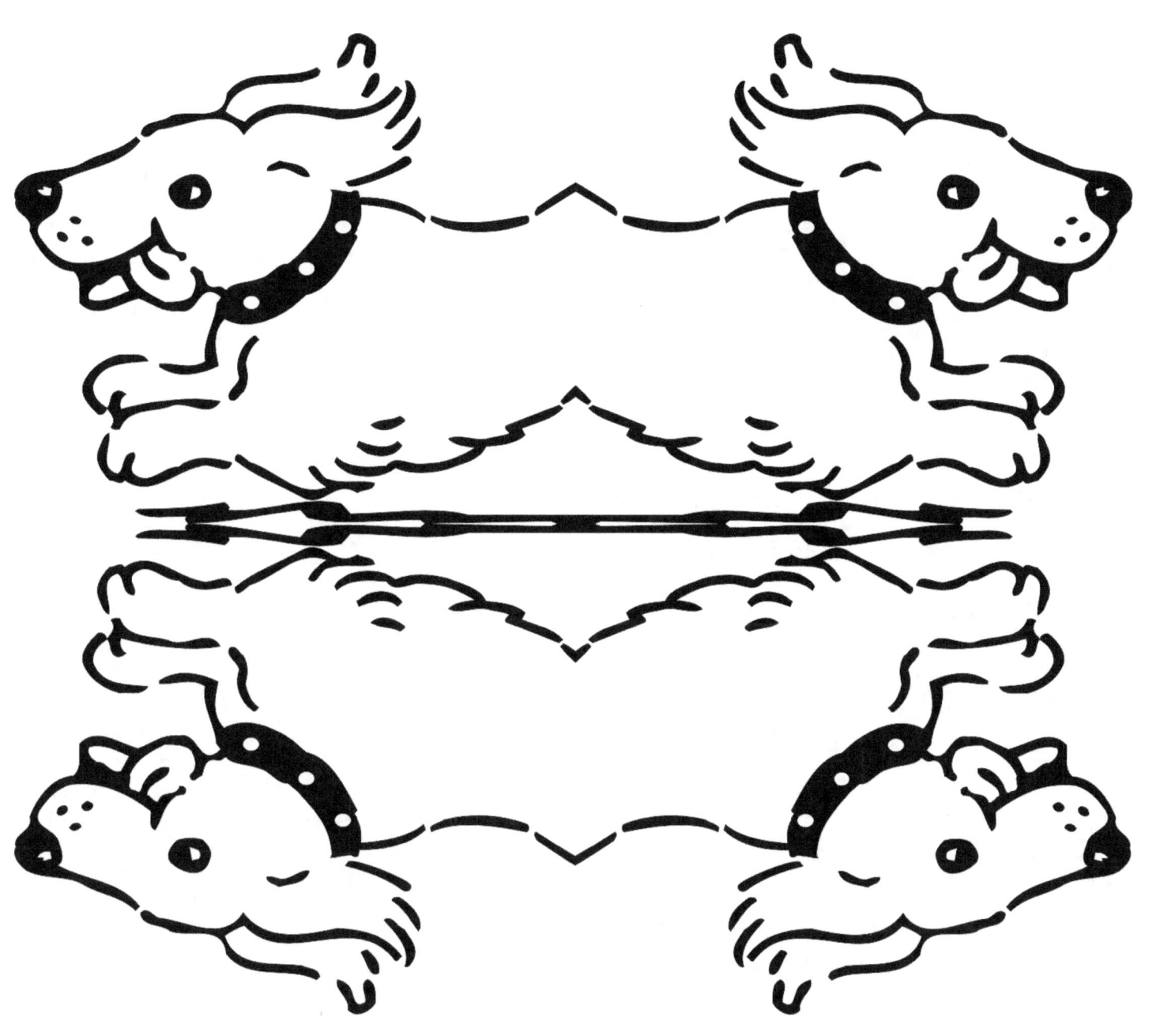

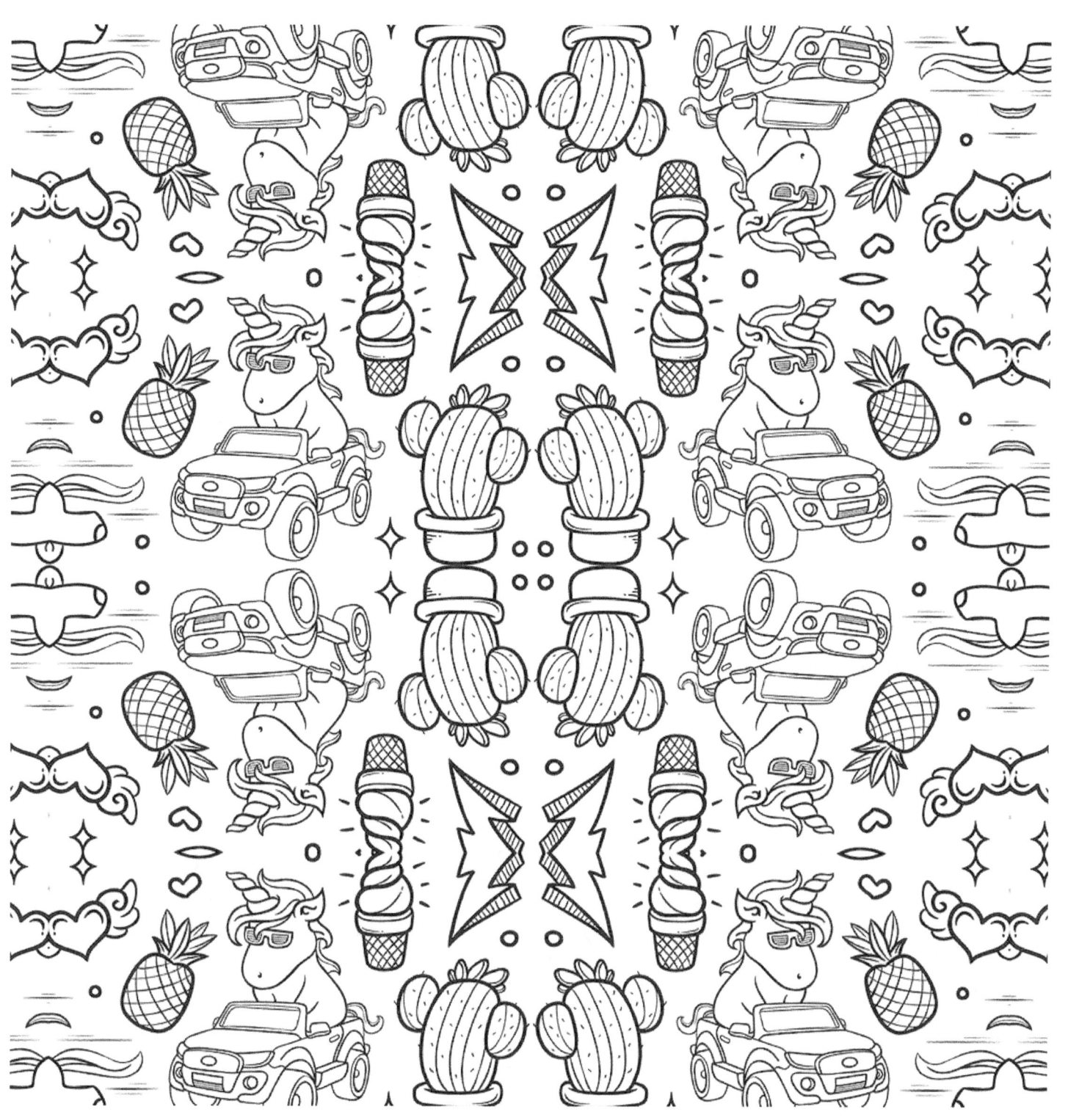

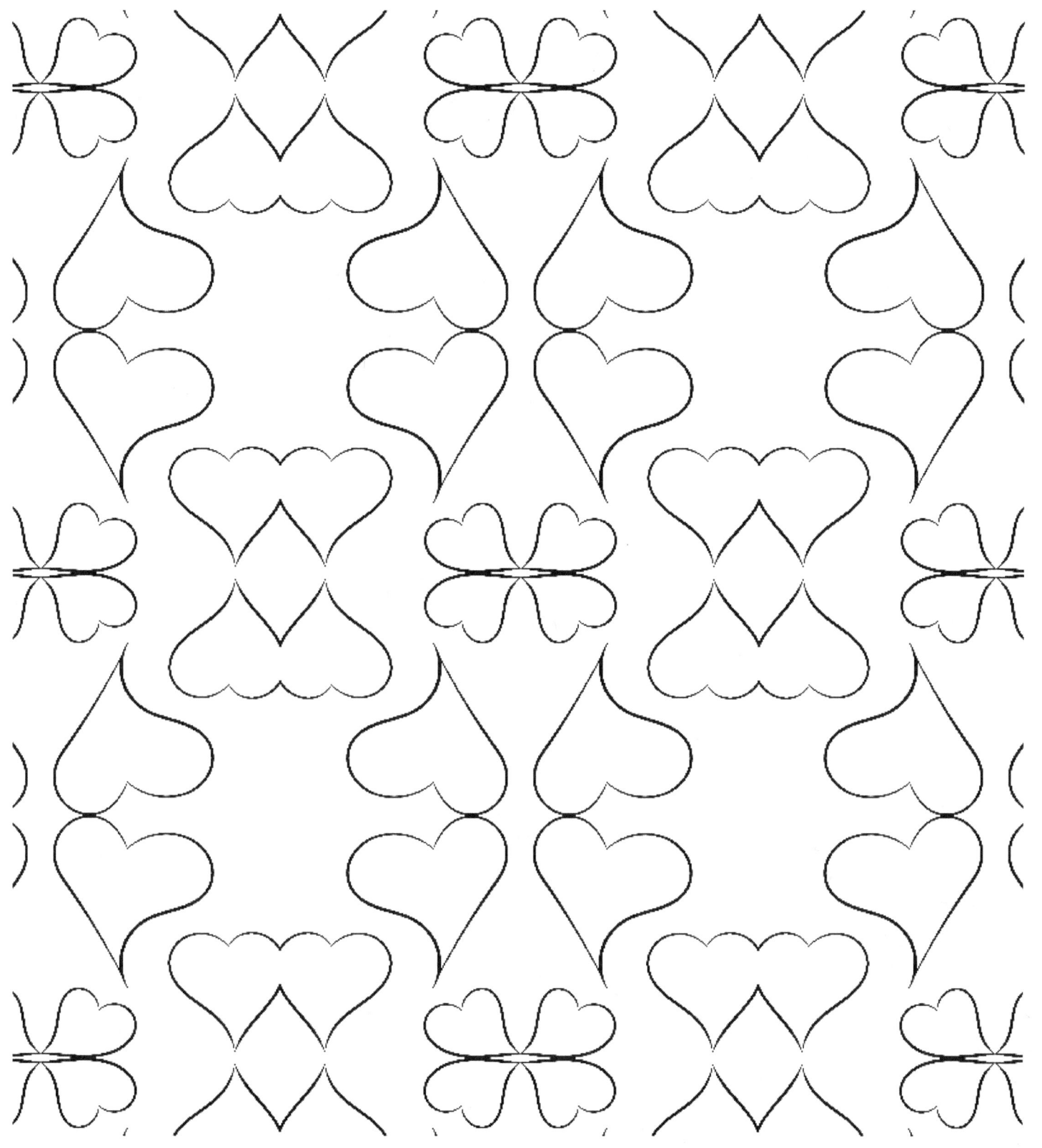

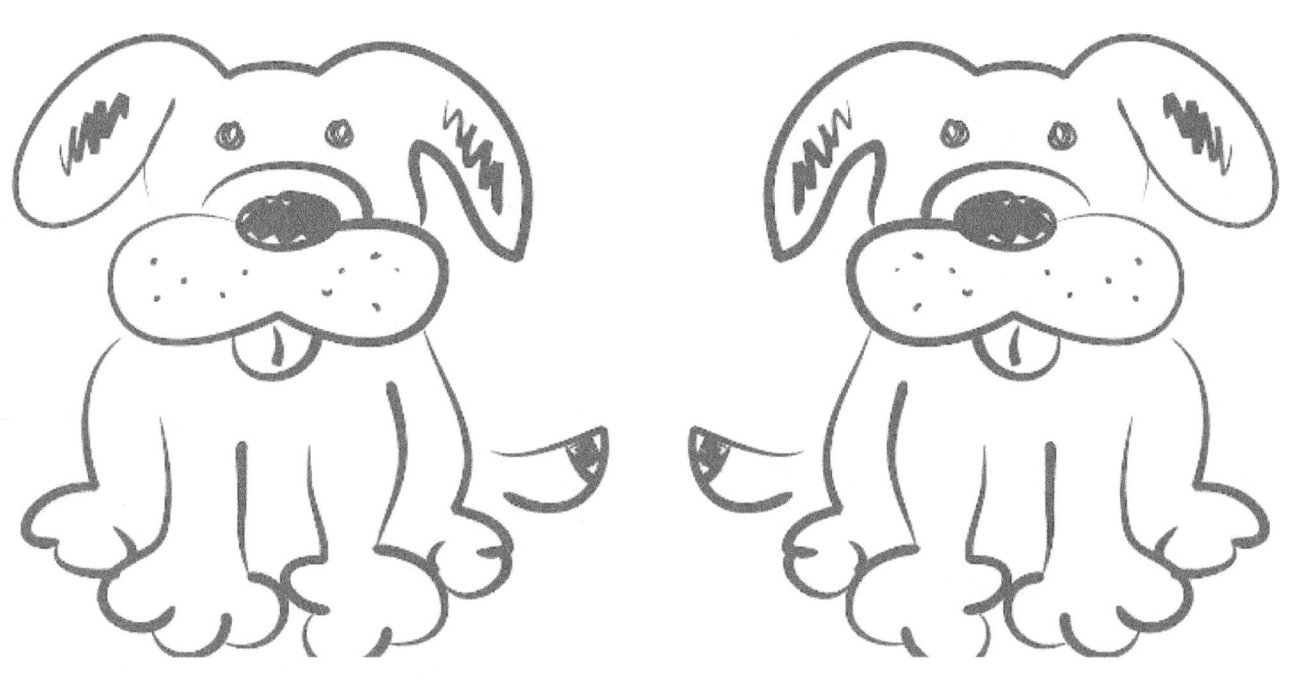

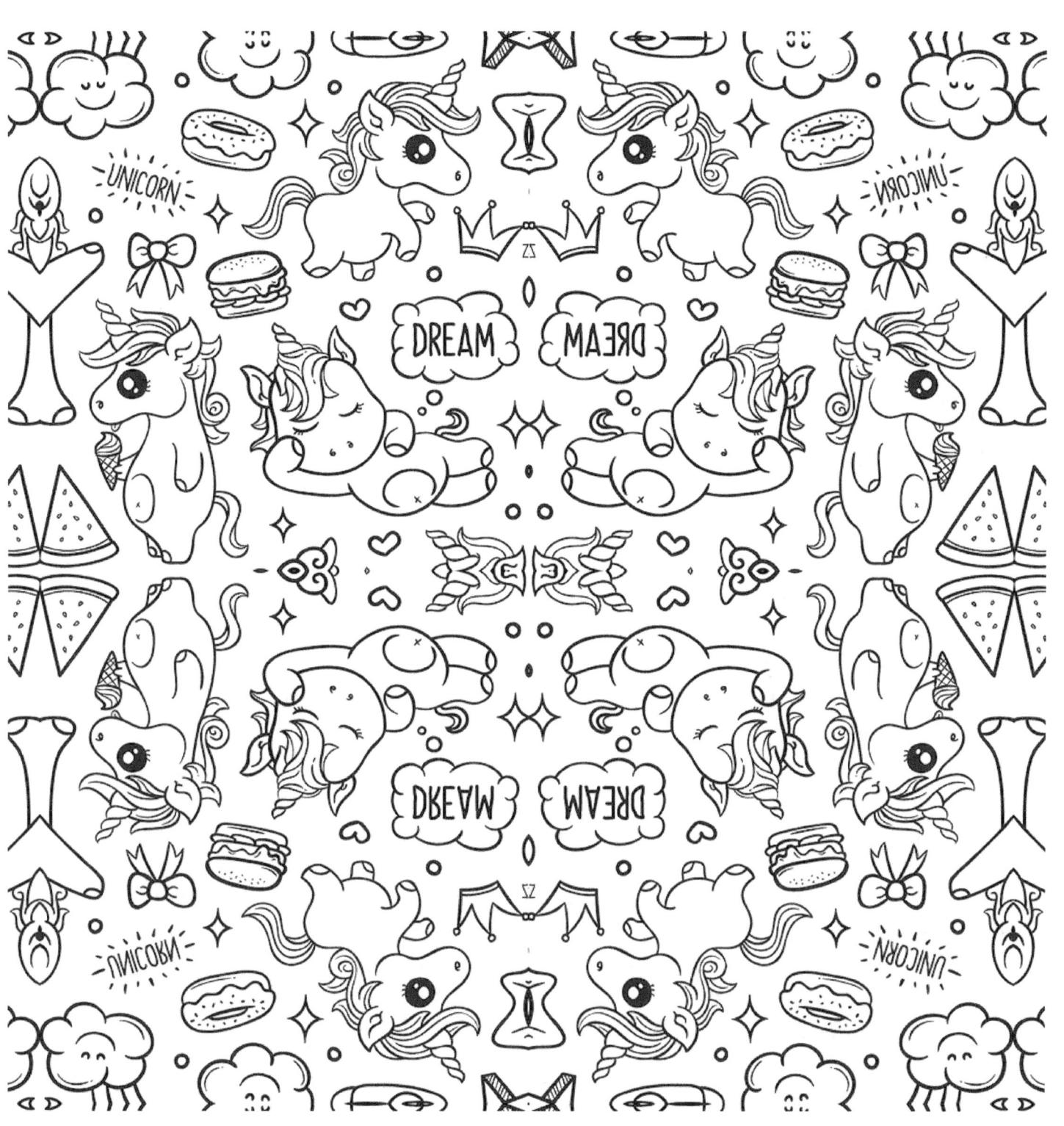

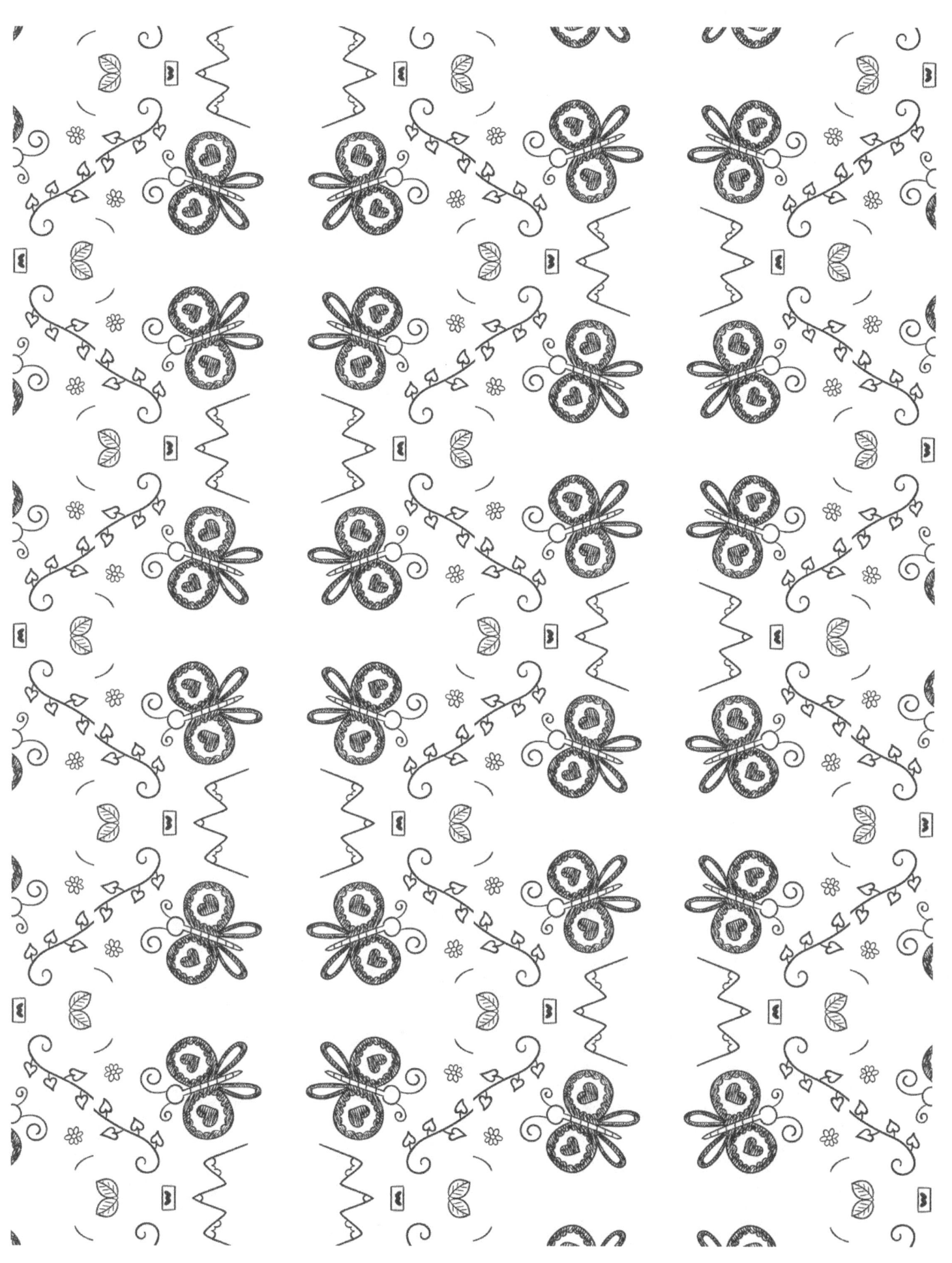

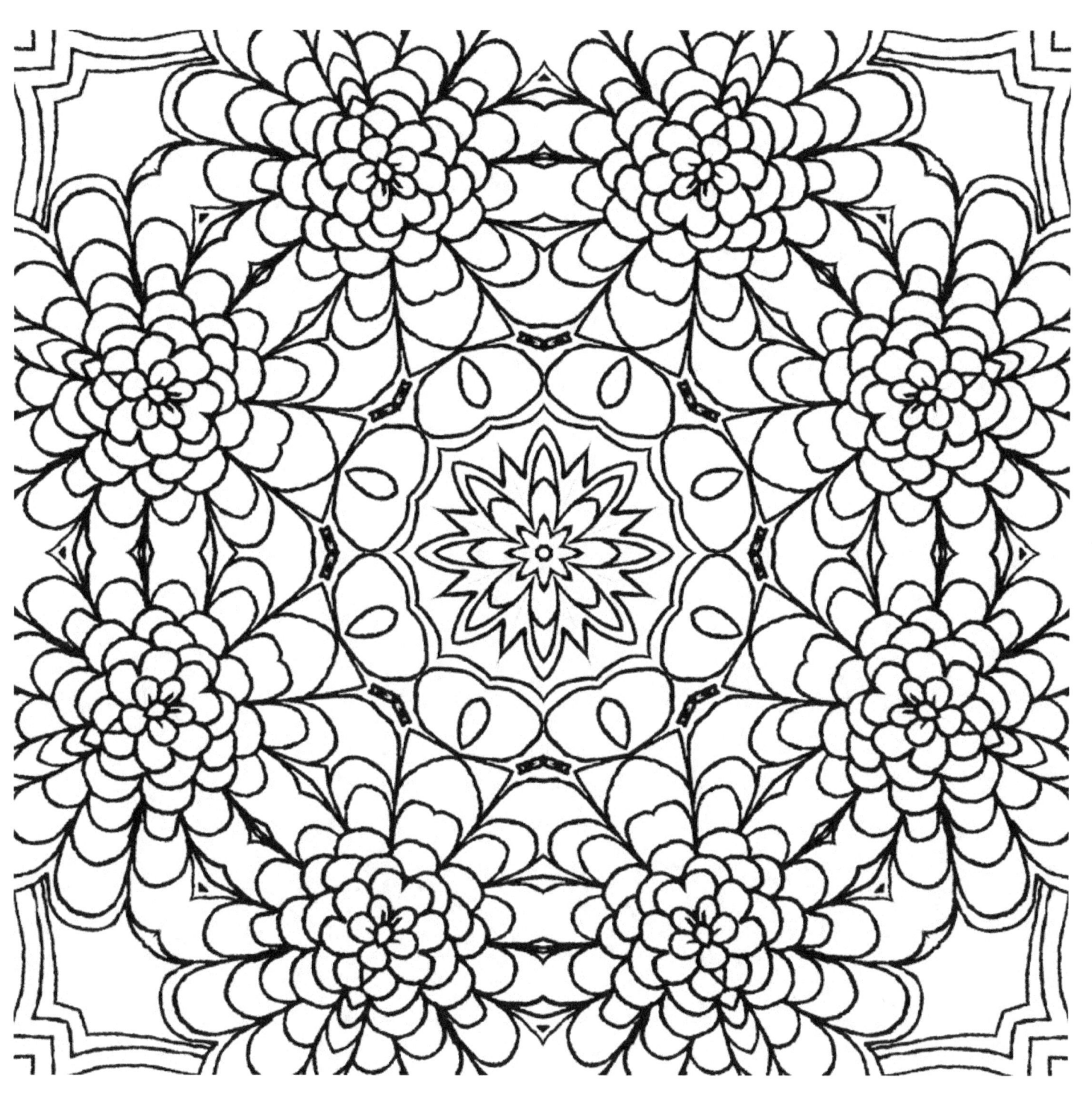

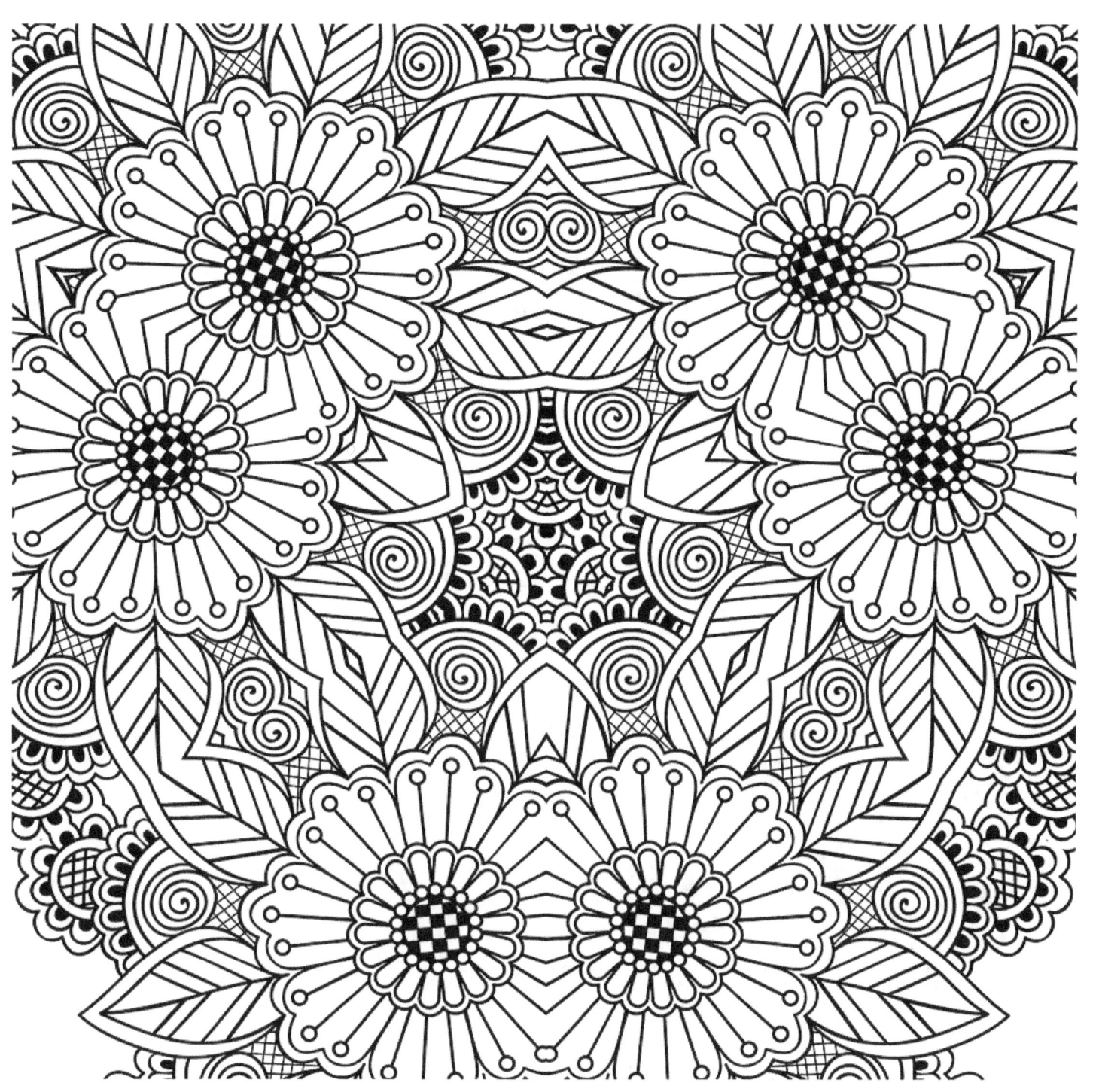

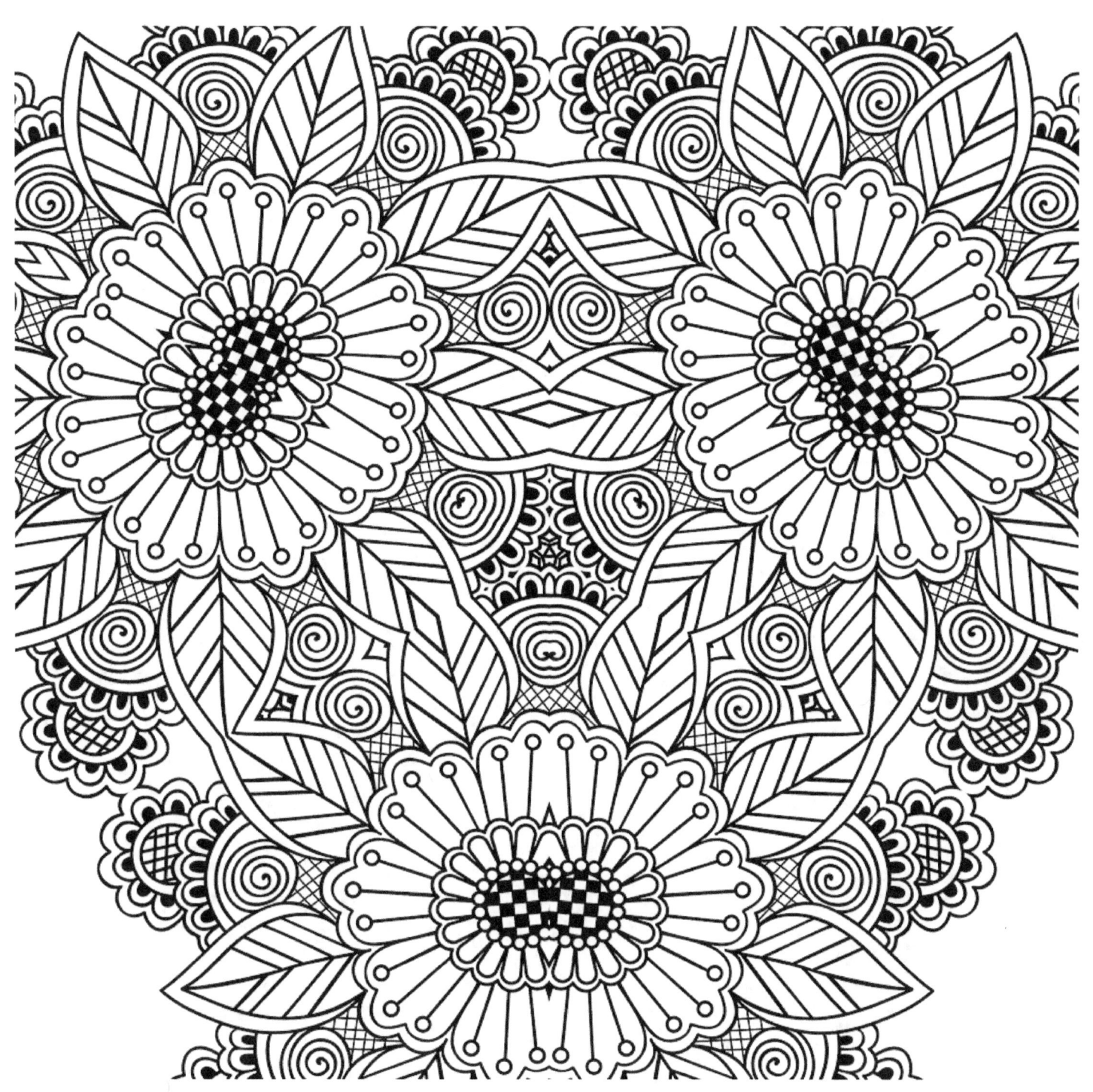

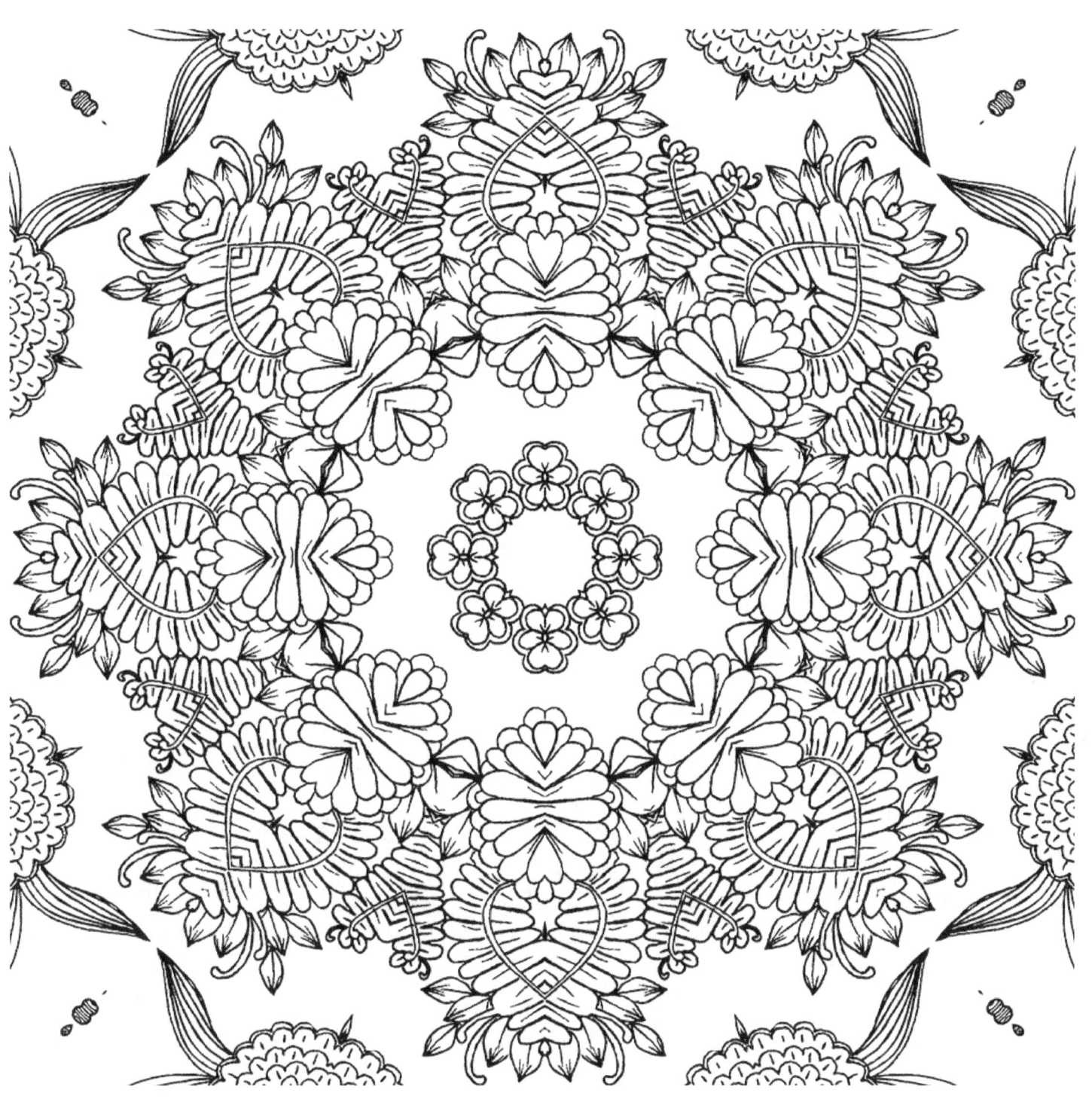

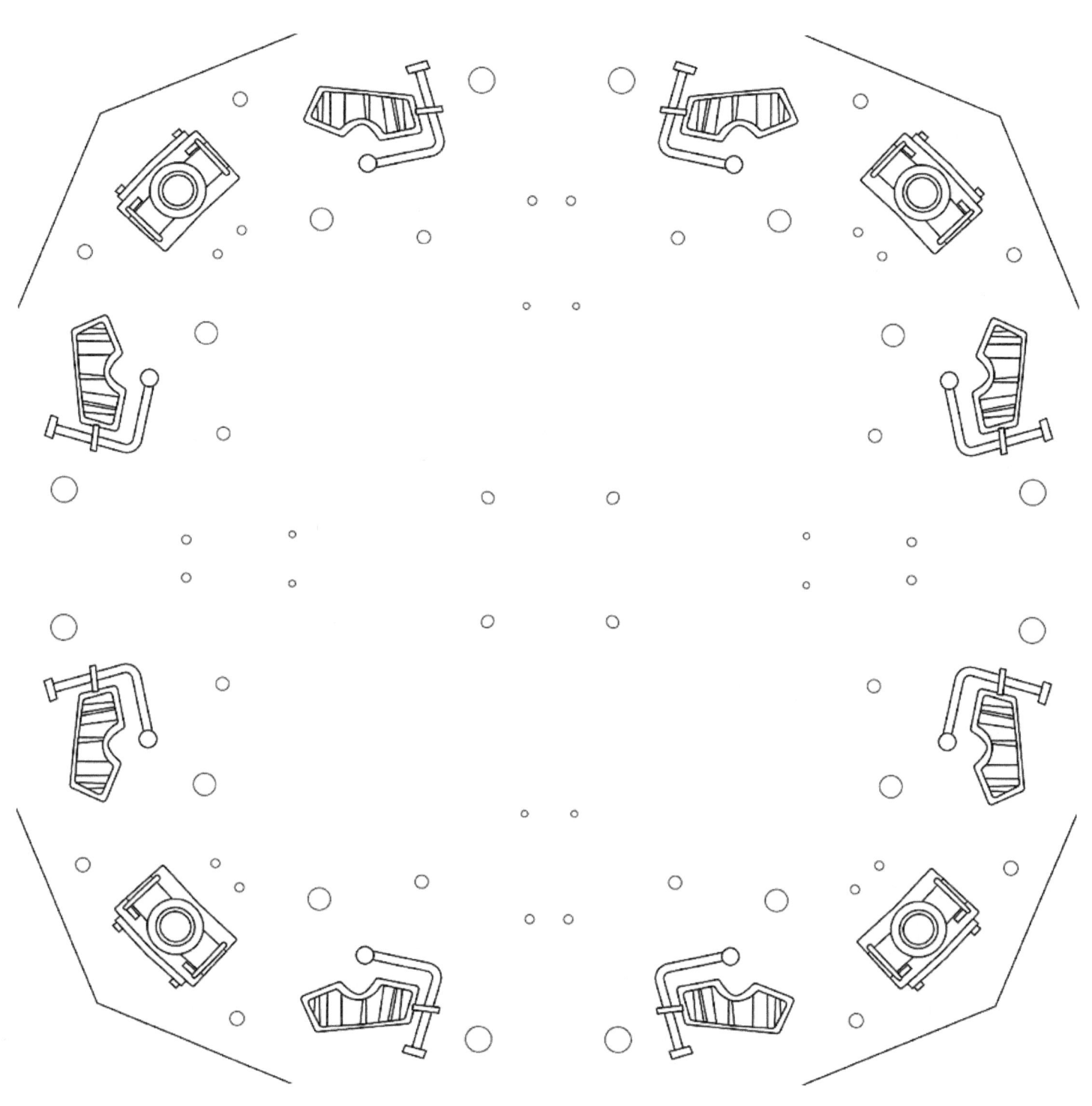

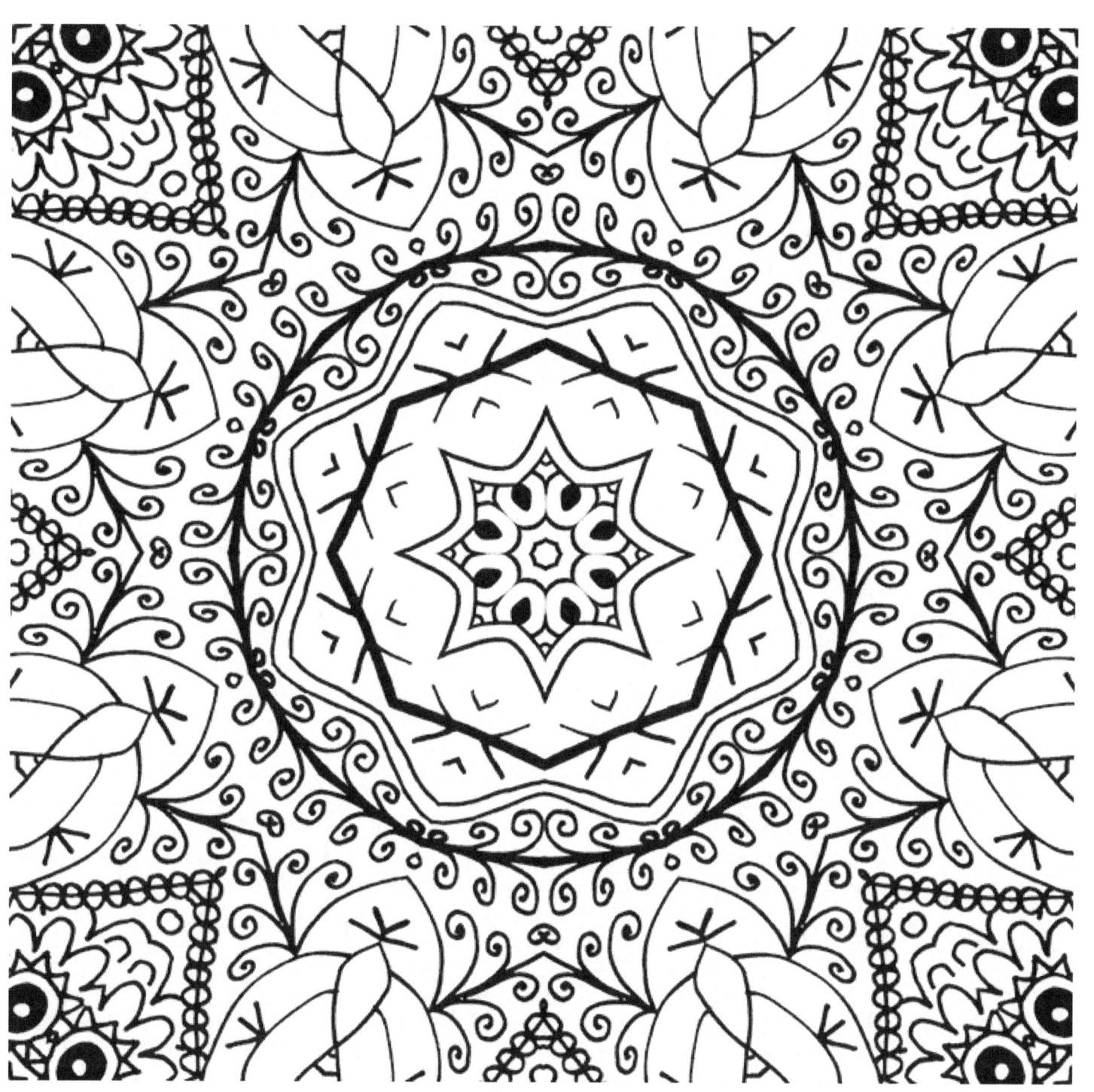

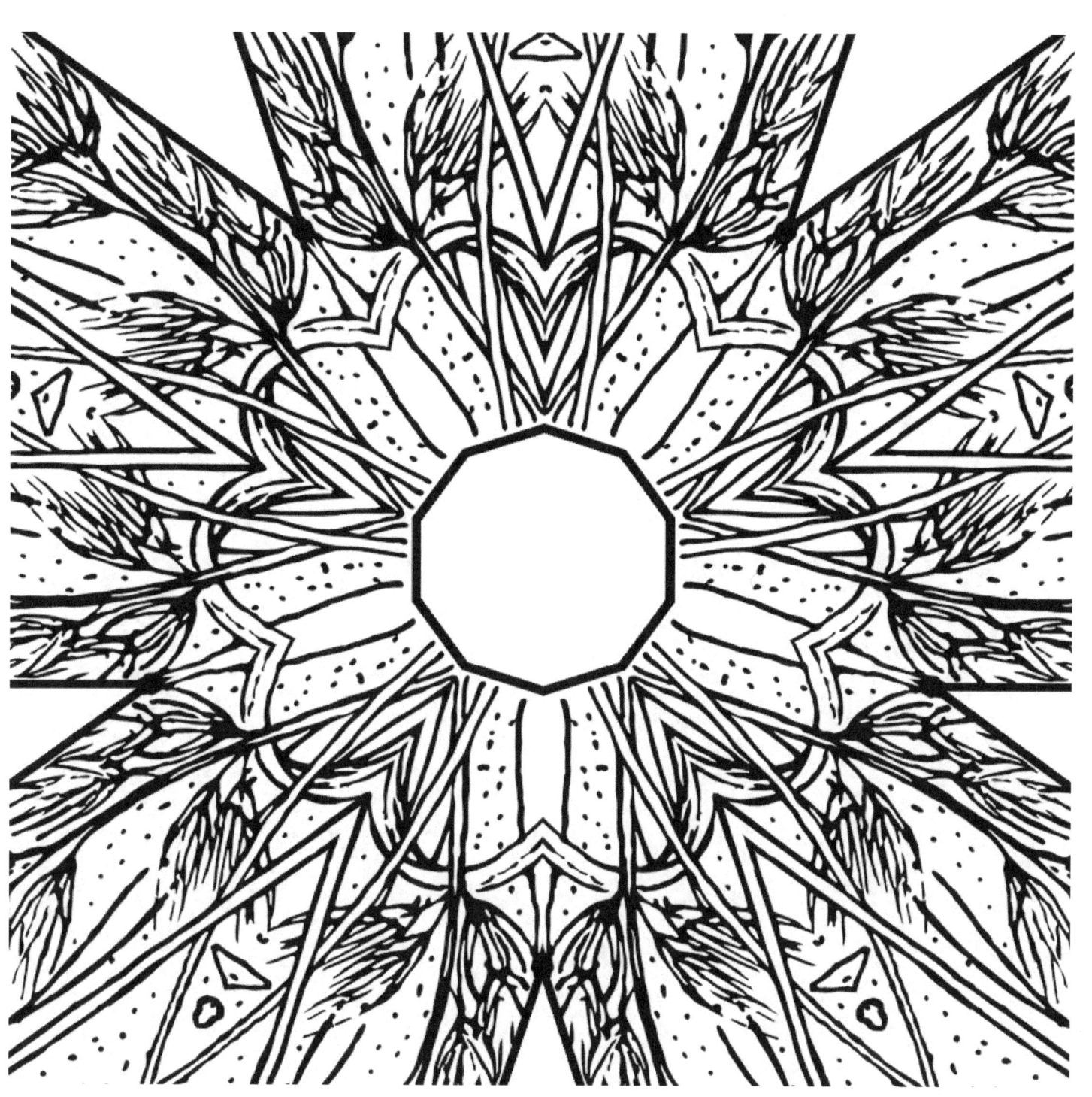

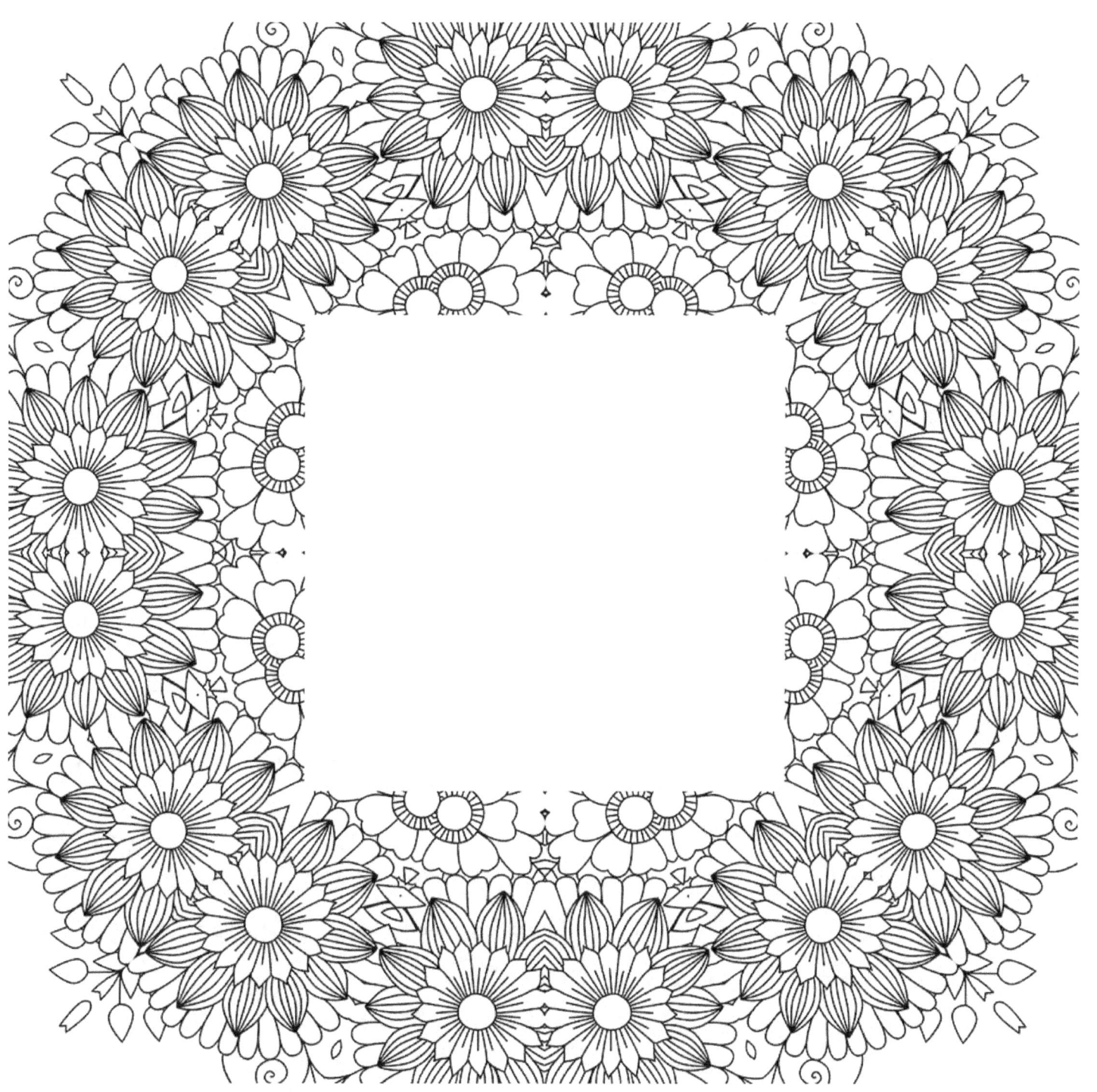

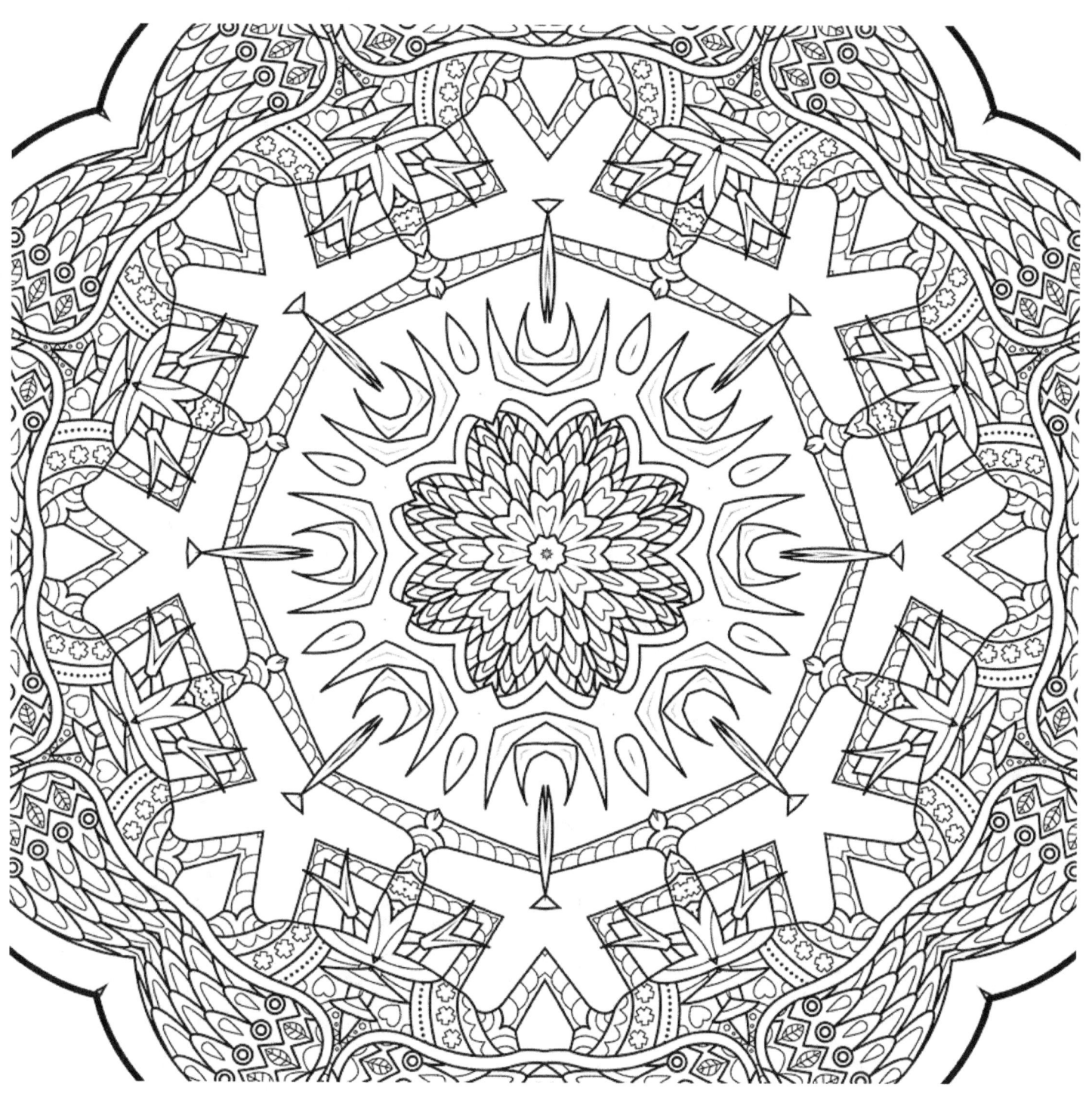

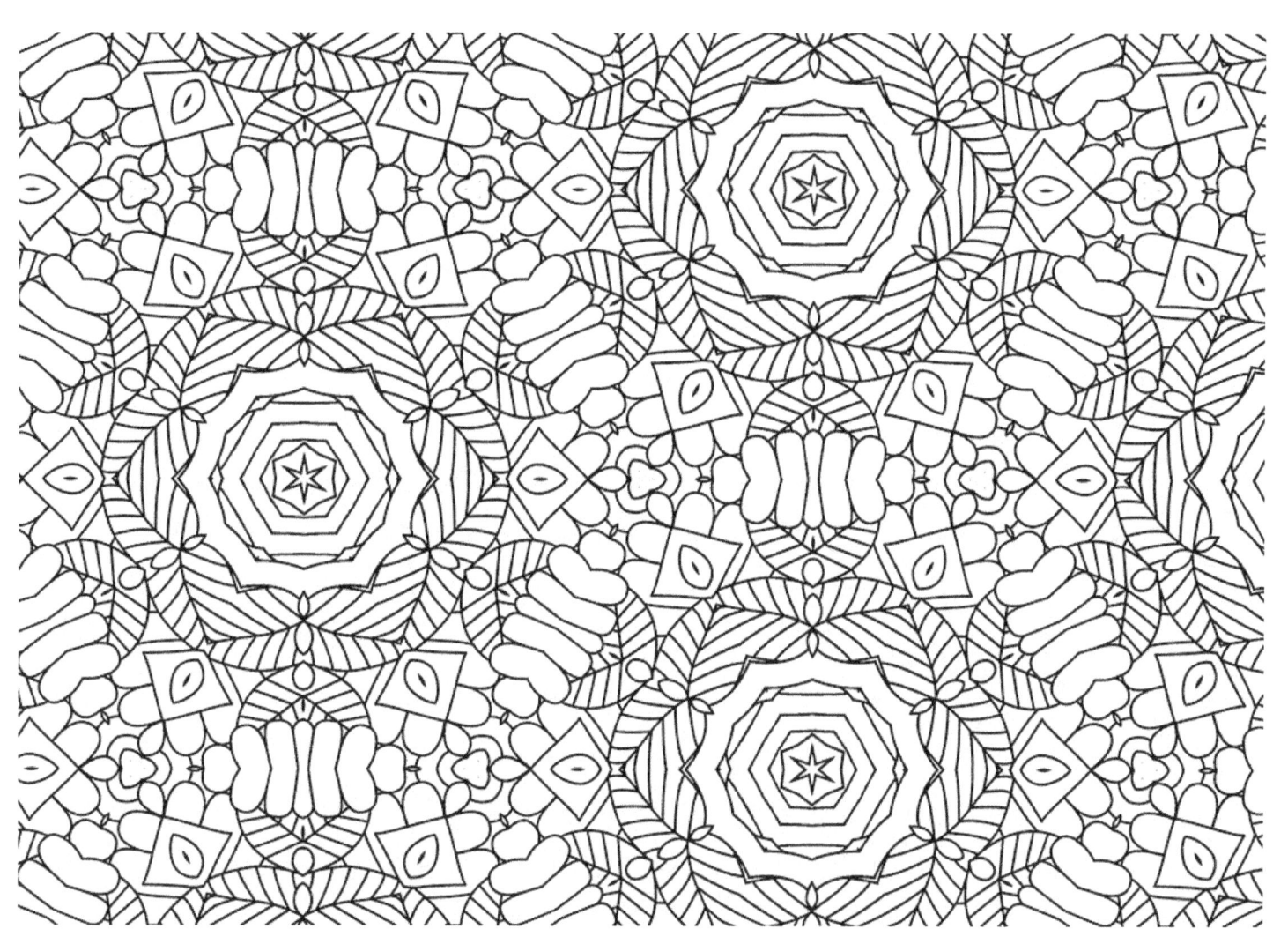

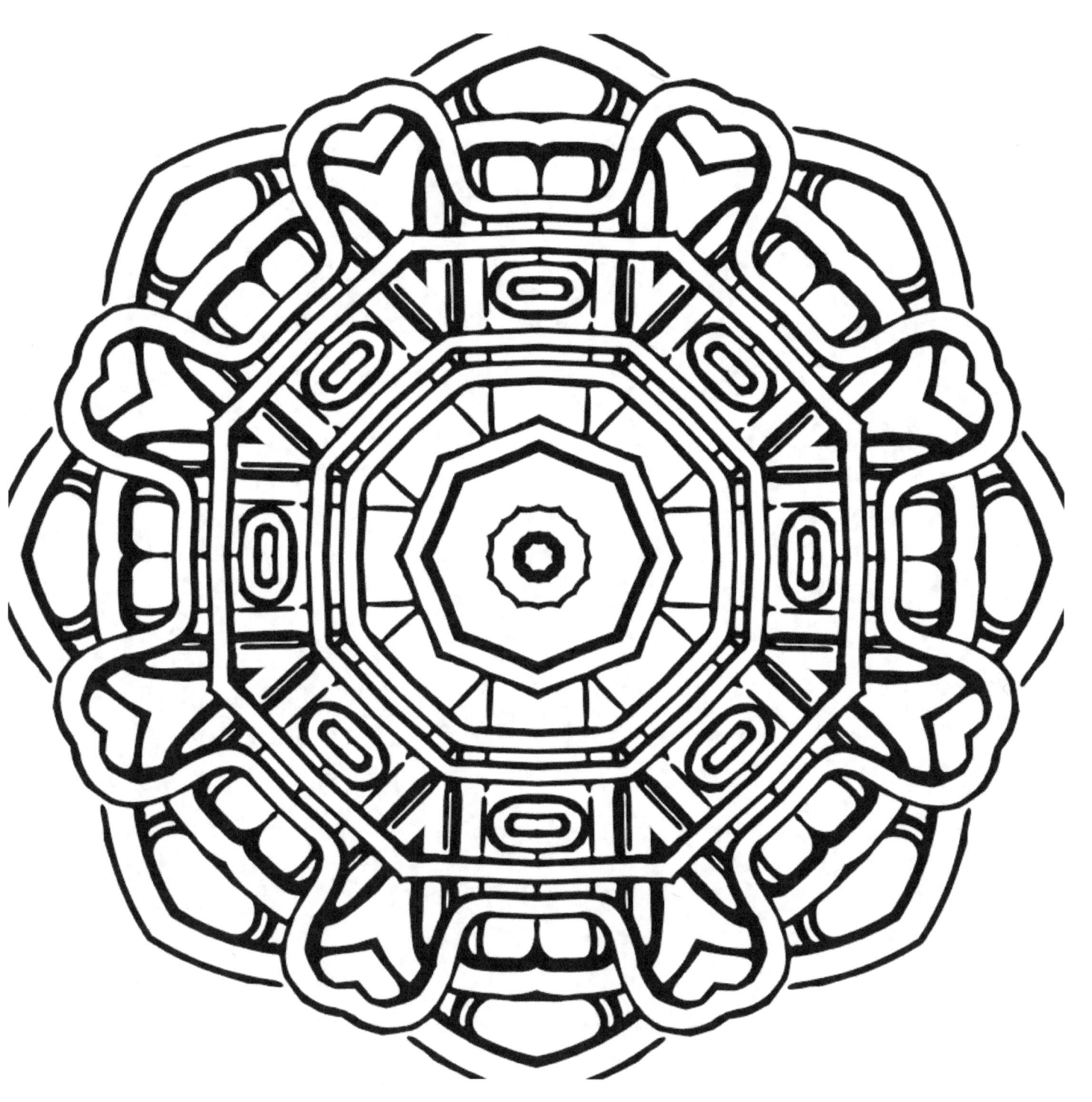

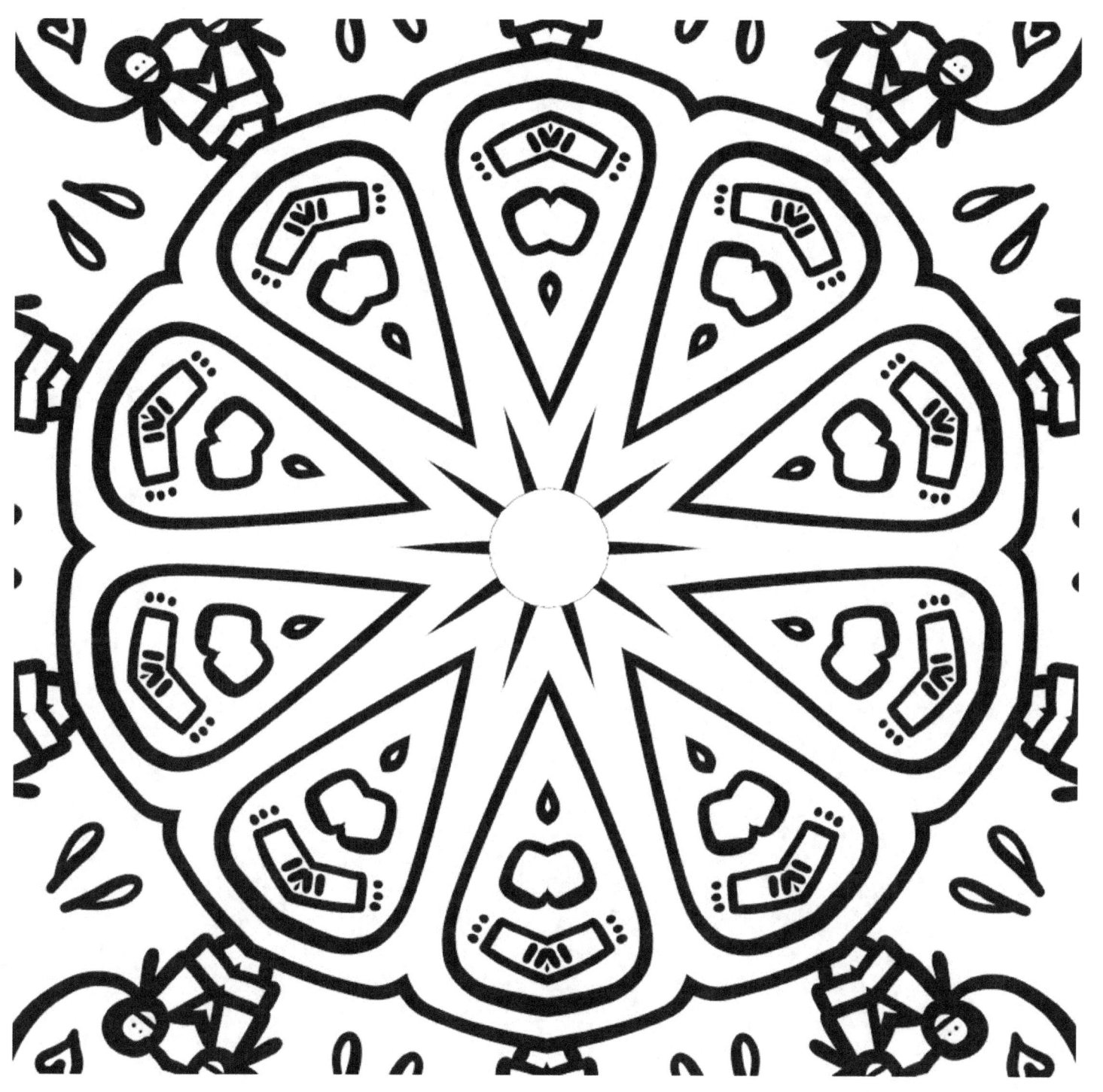

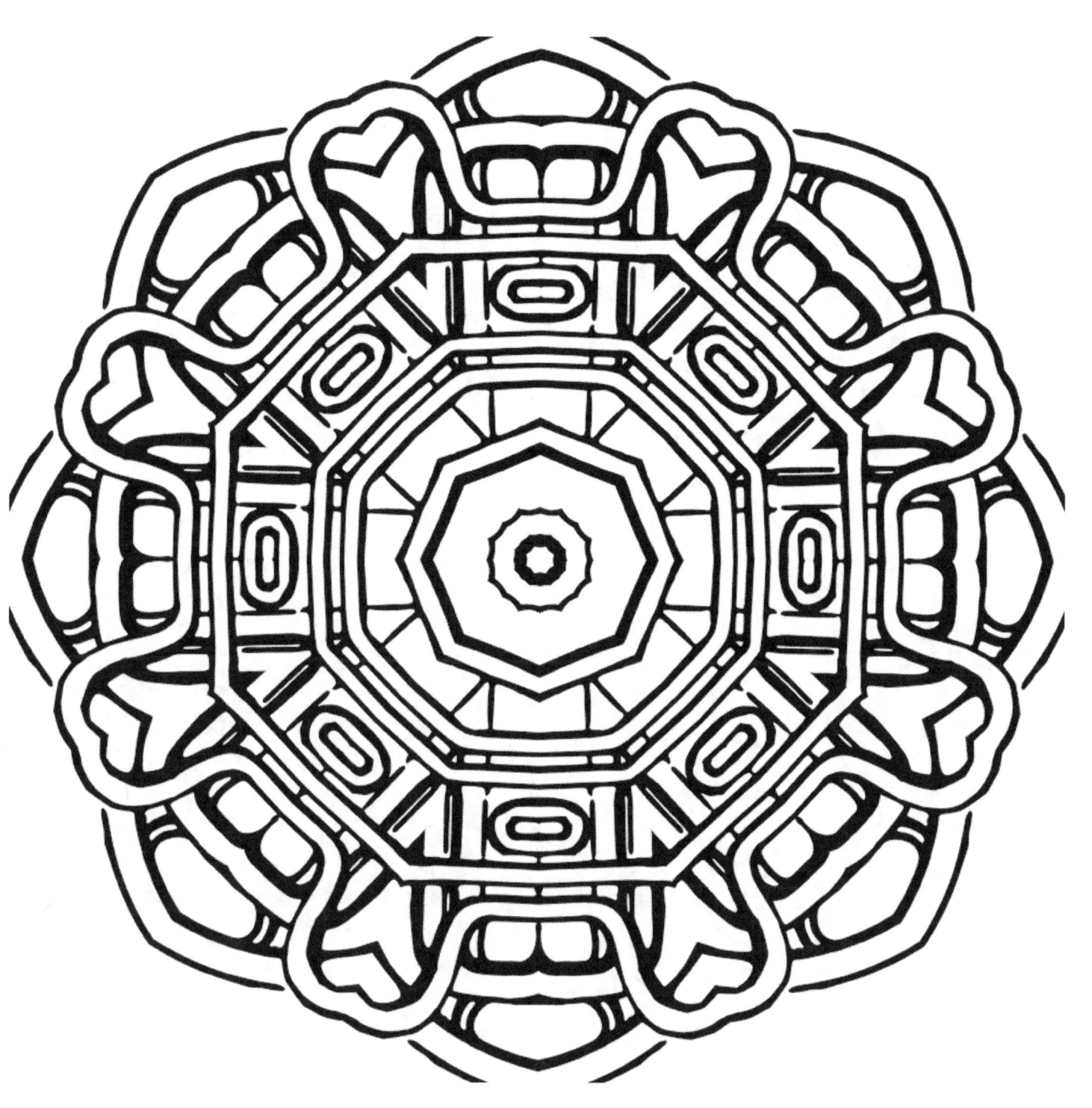

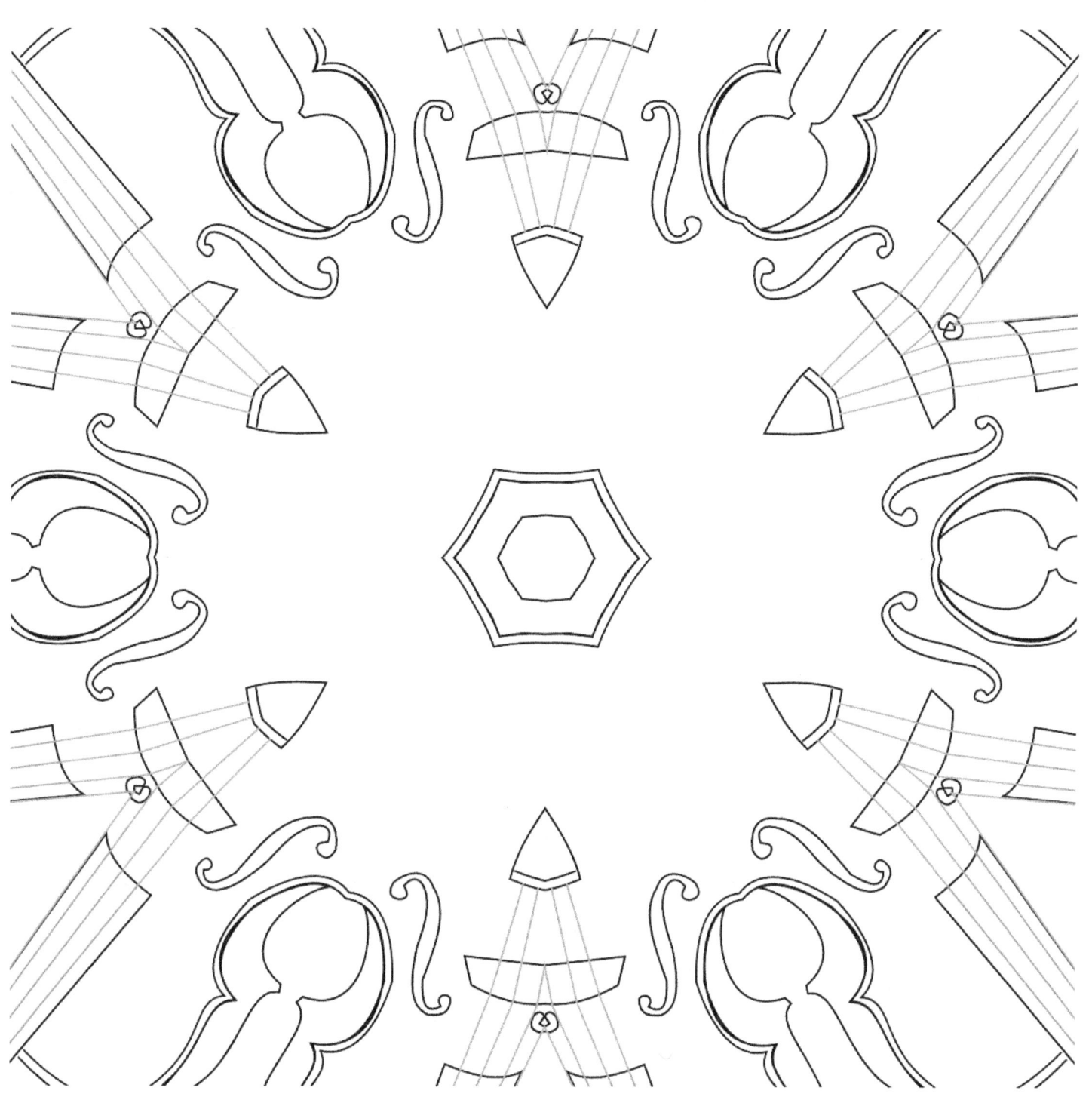

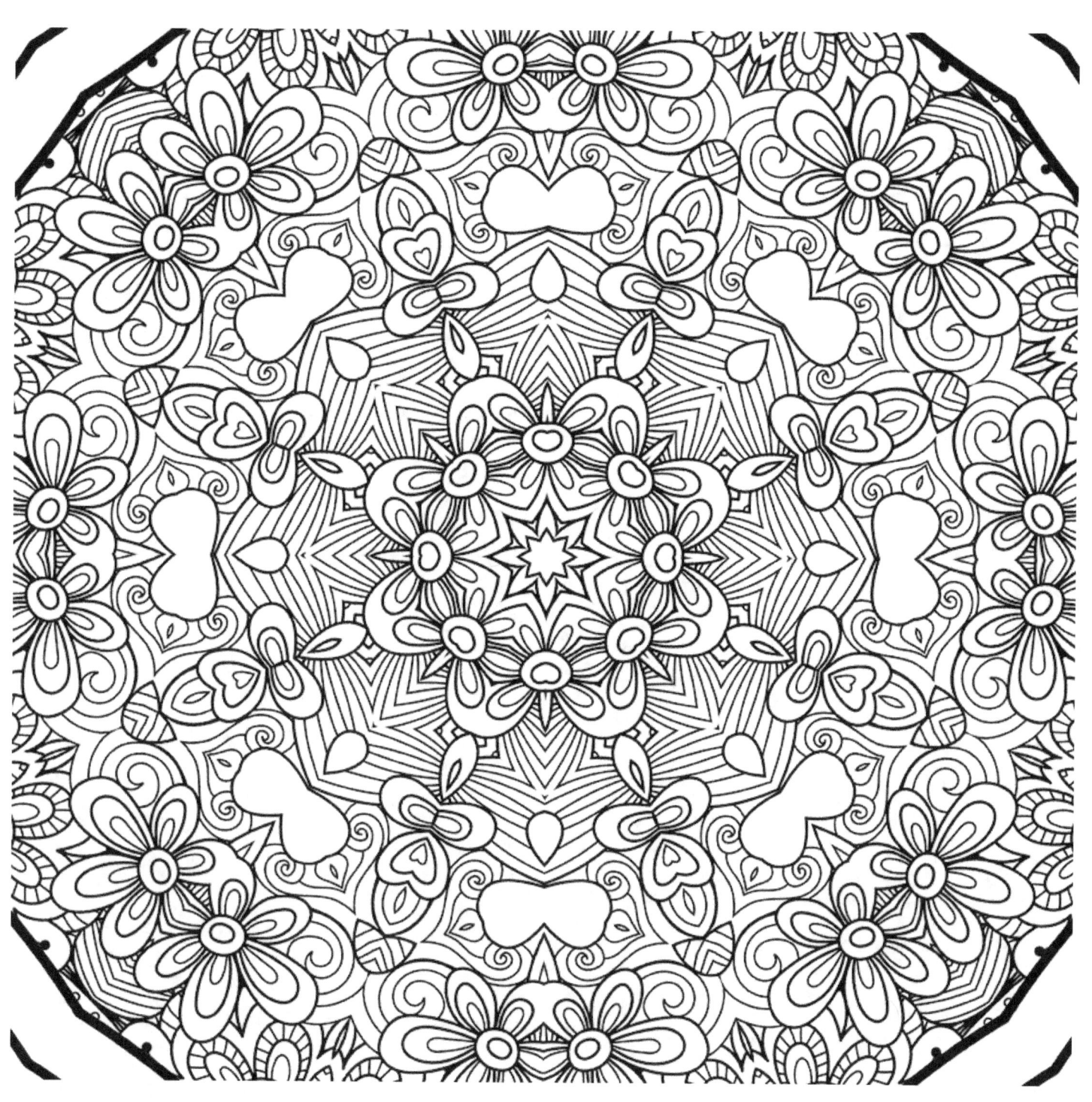

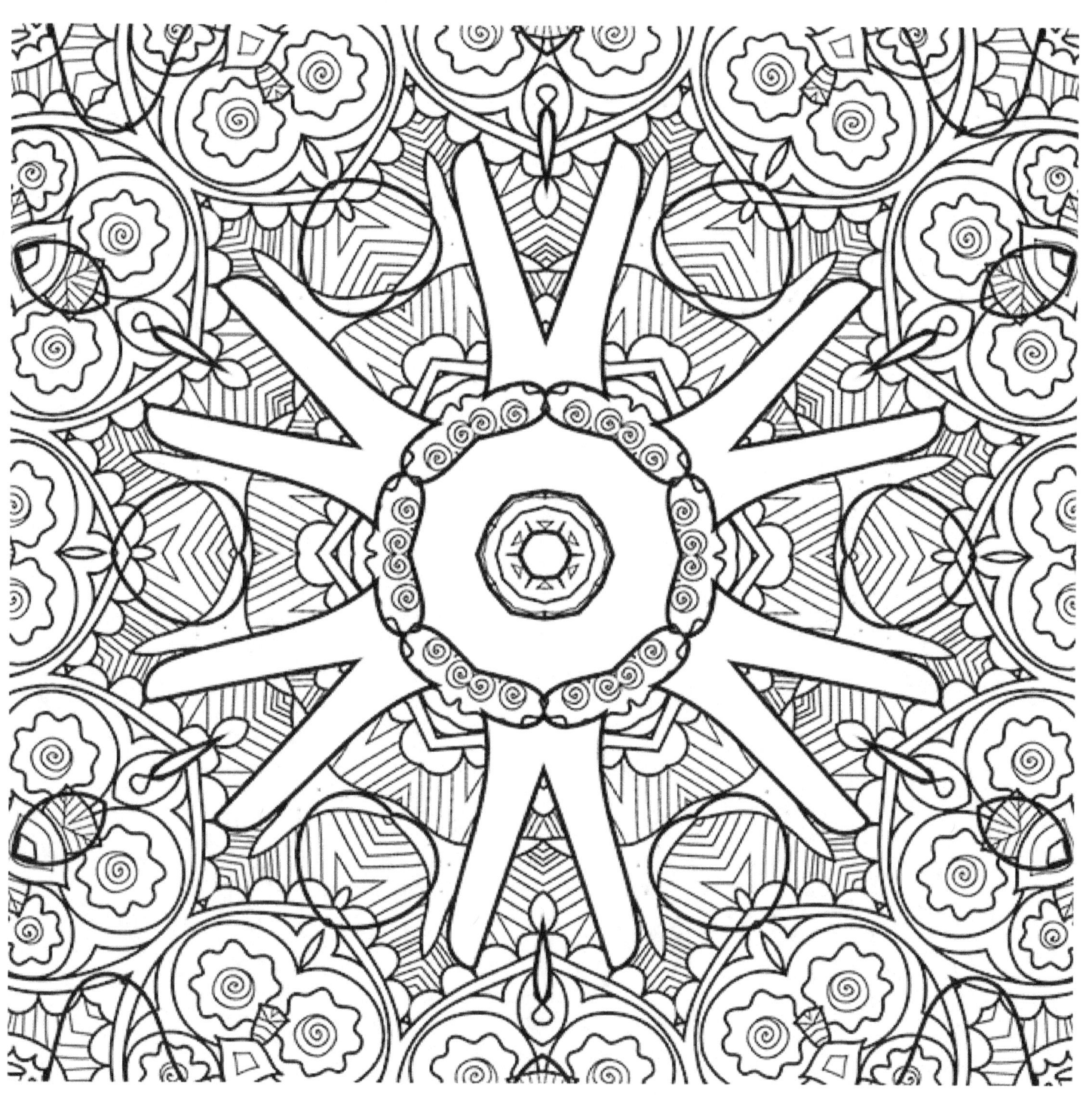

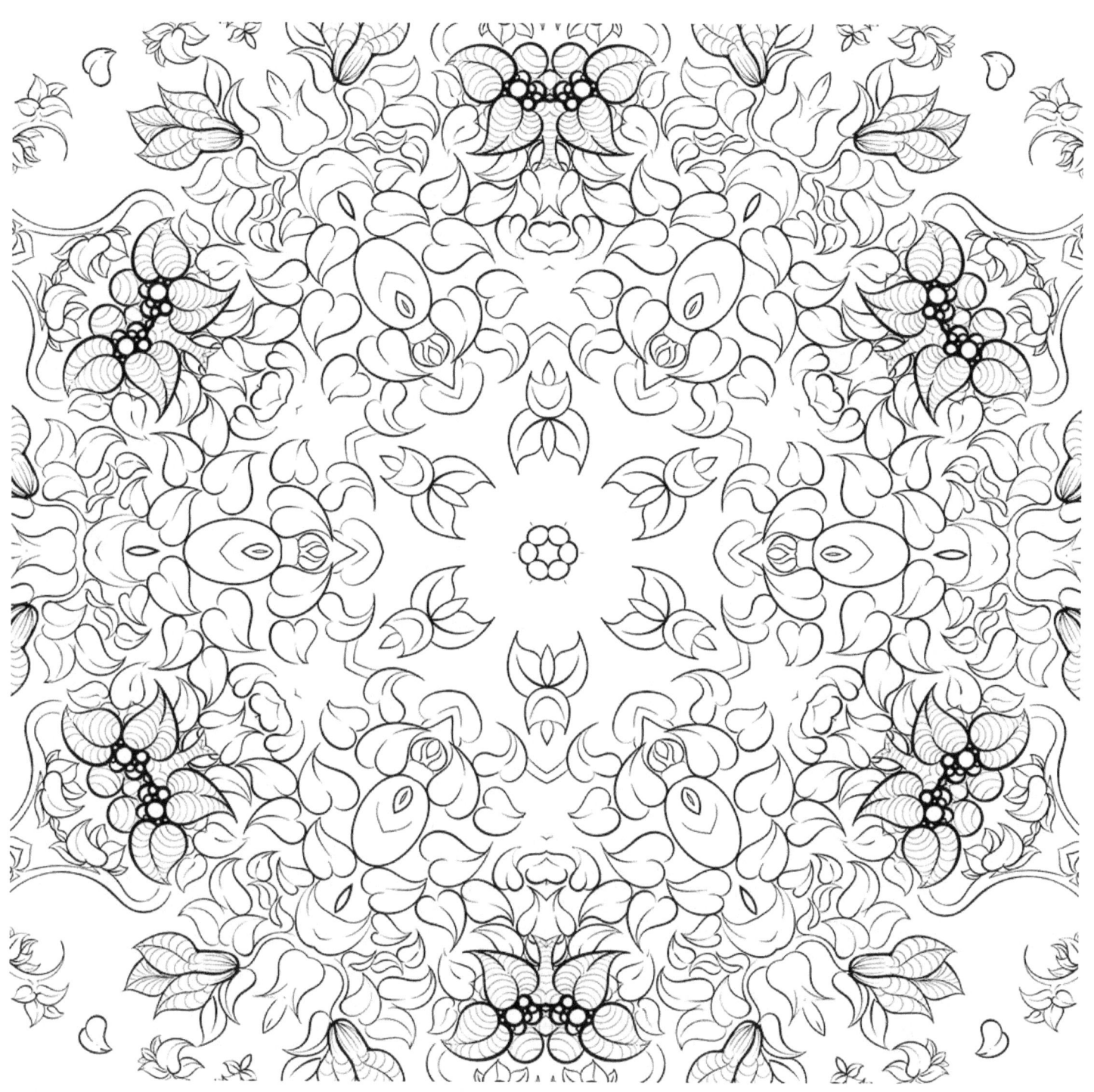

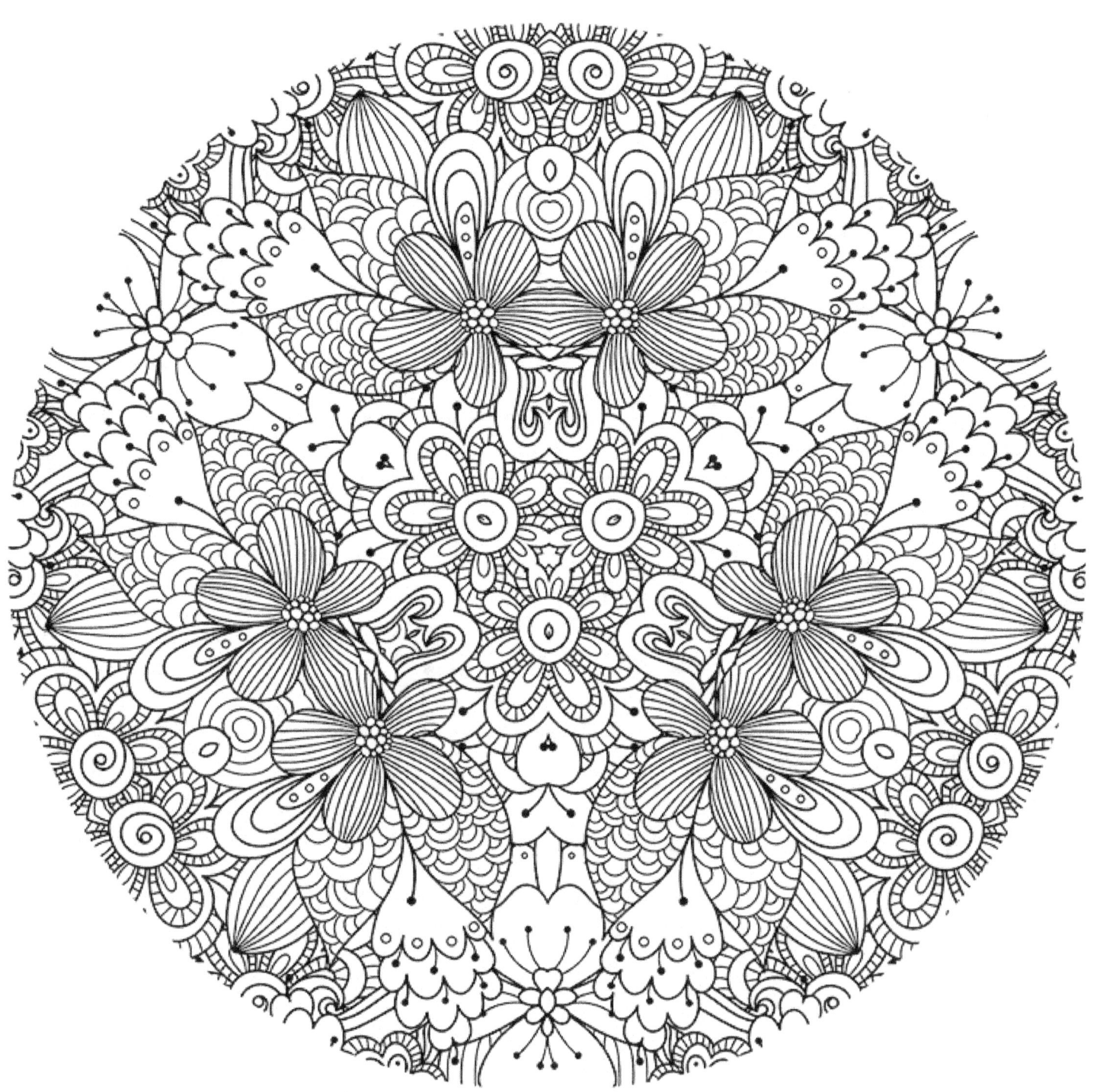

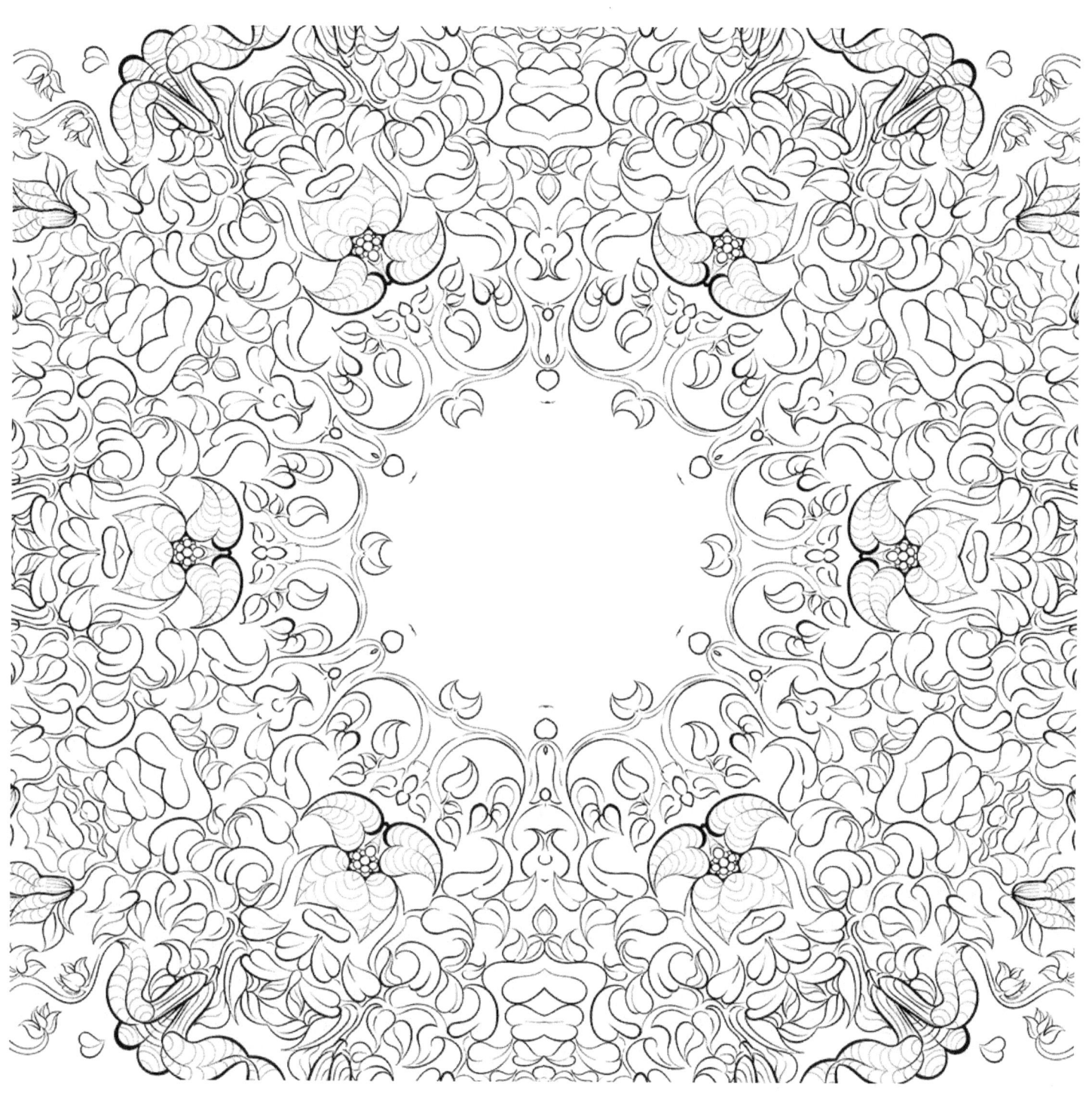

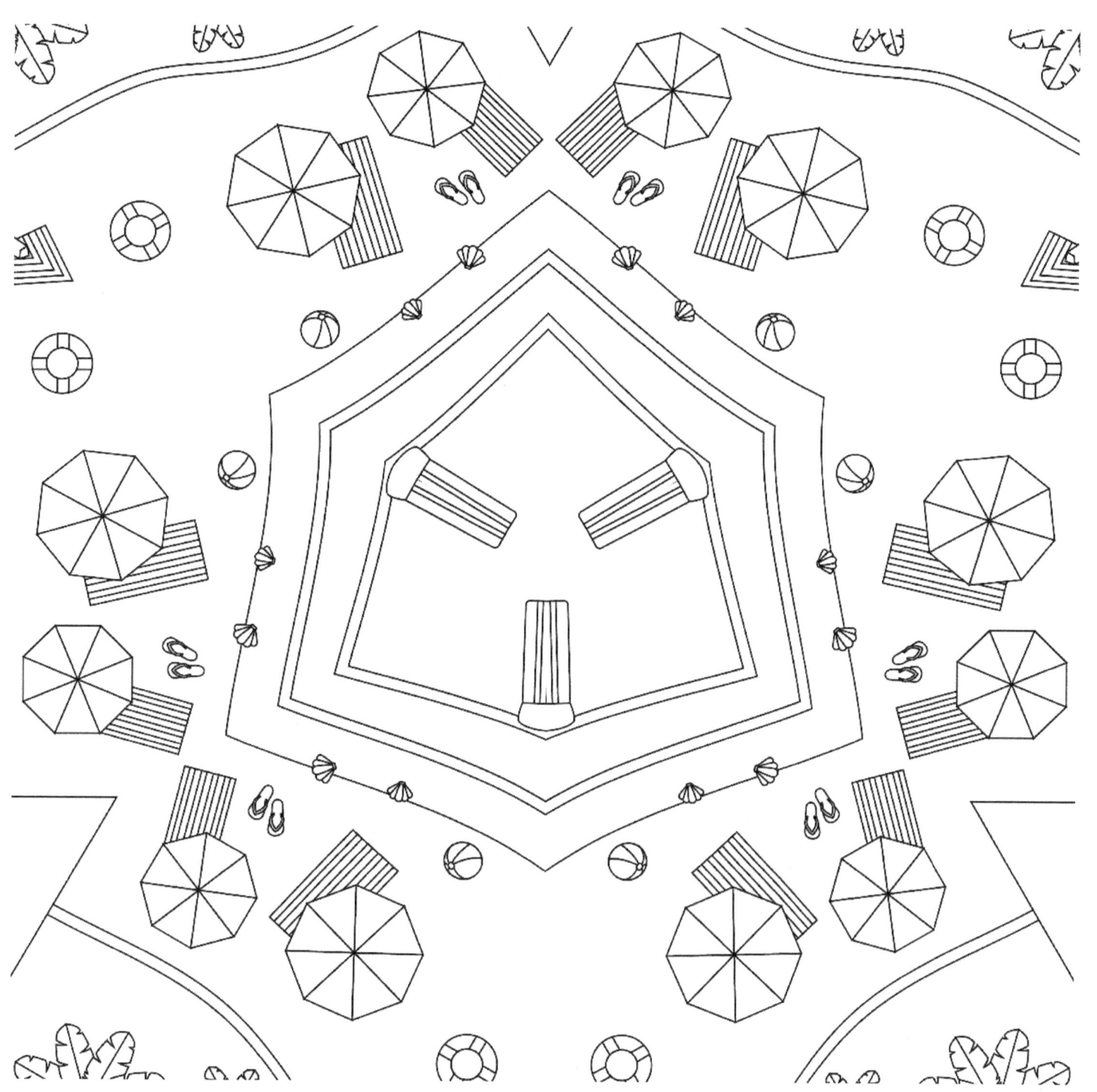

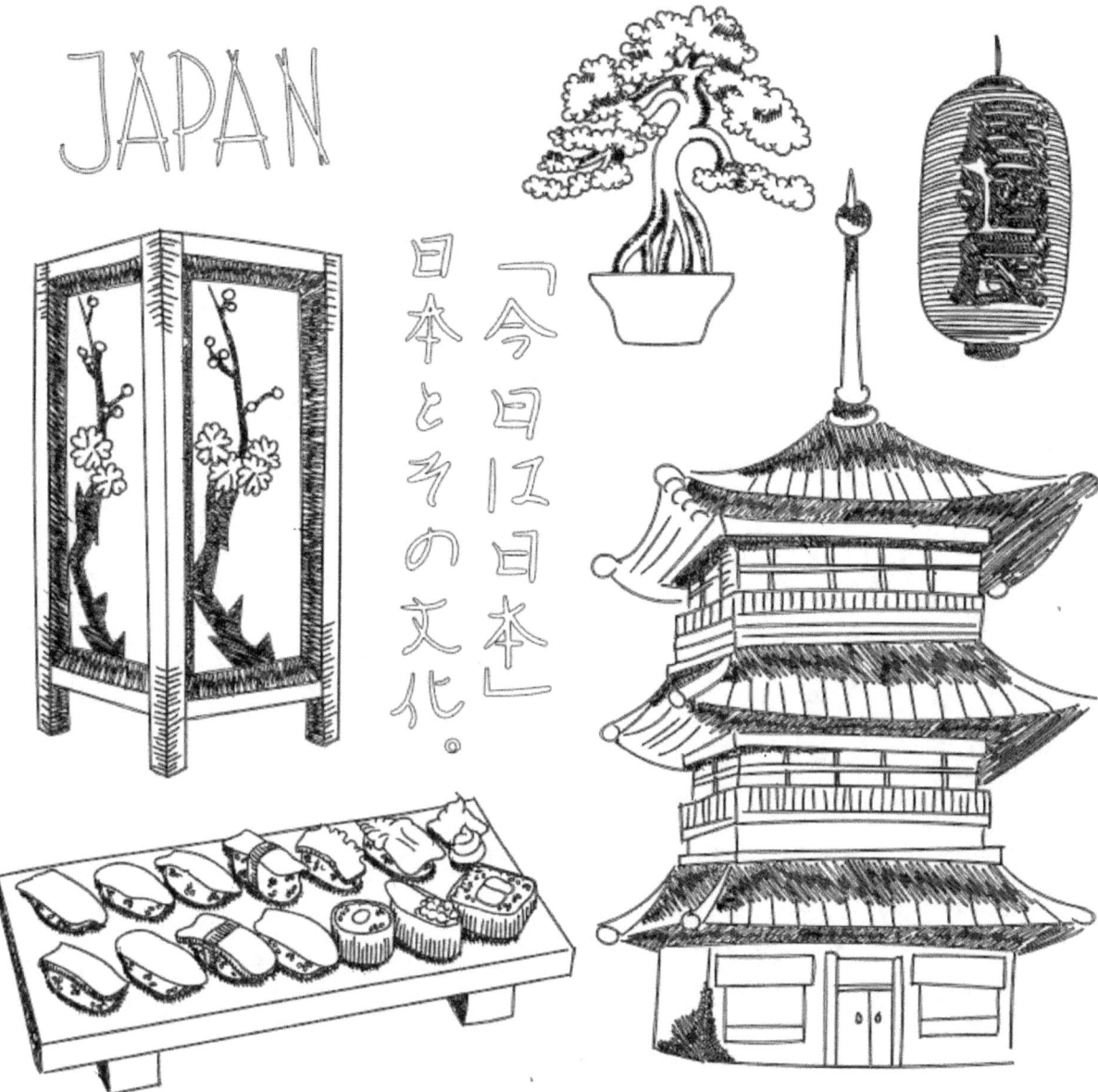

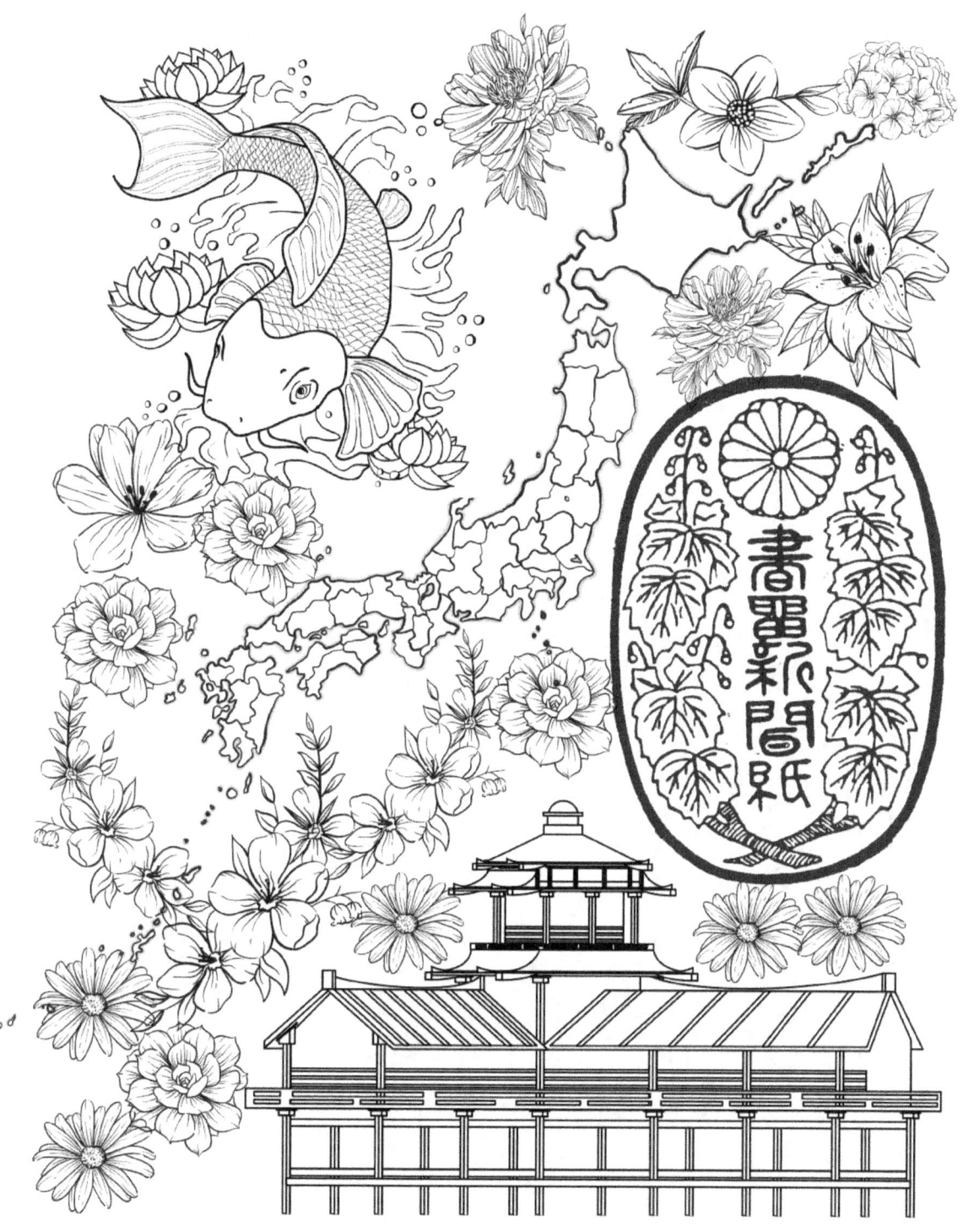

www.ingramcontent.com/pod-product-compliance
Lightning Source LLC
Chambersburg PA
CBHW081434220526
45466CB00008B/2387